NEW ORLEANS SCHOOL of COOKING

Across THE Table

Anne Leonhard & Harriet Robin

Text: Anne Leonhard & Harriet Robin
Project Coordinator: Jeanne Arceneaux Luna
Cover photograph: Matthew Noel
Back cover photograph: Stephen Luna
Food Photos: ©Ann Benoit & Thomas Dalferes
Ann Benoit Text & Image 2017
New Orleans photographs: Terry Thibeau
New Orleans photographs: Joyce Hanks
Book Design: Stephen Luna
Front Cover & Font Design: Ali Solino

First Printing, 2017
ISBN 978-0-692-83949-2

Printed in China

W I M M E R
cookbooks
wimmerco.com   800.548.2537

"Cookbooks of Distinction"™

NEW ORLEANS SCHOOL of COOKING

To find Joe's Stuff, Sliced Garlic and many more useful Louisiana cooking products to accompany these recipes, shop our New Orleans locations, our online store, or give us a call!

524 St. Louis Street
New Orleans, LA 70117
504.525.COOK
1.800.237.4841
www.neworleansschoolofcooking.com

Whether you take a class with us, shop our store, or use our products at home – visit the New Orleans School of Cooking as a guest, and leave as family.

Contents

Introduction

Food is love. Food is life. Food connects us to family and friends. And, food has taken us places we never, ever thought we would travel. Our journey through life has always involved food in one way or another. From those early years while juggling work and family, we both embraced our roles as mothers and head chefs of the household. Cooking was a necessity and really our second job, a job we both enjoyed and embraced. Little did we know years later we would reinvent ourselves and our lives and become the official New Orleans Grannies! Cooking throughout the years enabled us to create memories around events with family and friends. We share special recipes and techniques taught to us by our own grandmothers, mothers, aunts, friends and neighbors. Even though we are definitely two distinctive ladies - a robust, outspoken maven and a fiery petite redhead - as native New Orleanians we share a common bond that starts in the kitchen.

Revealing that we grew up together in the New Orleans Lakeview neighborhood explains a lot. We are simpatico. In particular, we share the same values about life and family, and we both love New Orleans. It's our shared love of our city that seemingly encouraged our paths to cross and weave in and out of each other's lives for more than sixty-five years. While we saw each other at our children's school events and both even donated our time to bake sales and PTA, it wasn't until we became instructors at the New Orleans School of Cooking that we became a part of each other's lives again. Individually, our lives have grown by leaps and bounds through our experiences with Greg and Suzanne Leighton and the team at the New Orleans School of Cooking. We both had professional careers in our chosen fields, public school education and dietetics and nutrition. And, we both cultivated people of all ages to learn and grow along with us. It is most fitting that we have found a voice again teaching and mentoring but this go round focused on our beloved New Orleans food culture.

Individually, we share our stories and techniques every week in the French Quarter culinary classrooms at the New Orleans School of Cooking. Most importantly, we both focus on what it takes to cook quintessential New Orleans dishes. Literally, we stand in front of thousands of peoples from across the United States and the world every year. When you get us together in the classroom, well quite frankly, that's when the real magic happens.

Literally, between the two of us, we have about 100 years of cooking experience.

Neither one of us grew up with a silver spoon in our hands – rather, ours was a wooden spoon! Cooking was a practical skill that we embraced when life and family called. We didn't grow up eating out. We grew up eating in! Cooking didn't really kick in for us until we had families of our own, simply because both of our mothers were handling things. Cooking was a practical necessity that over the years has become a love and an obsession. Because of our shared experiences, you put us in front of a stove with onions, bell peppers, celery and anything else you have on hand, and we can literally finish each others thoughts and recipes. Together, we create dishes that will make you wish you were part of our family. These recipes are dishes we grew up eating all our lives. Heaven only knows where our families and friends learned them. Some may even have come from cookbooks, magazines or newspapers. The people who gave them to us either don't remember or they're not with us anymore. Regardless of the origins, we have no intention of copying someone else's work.

Throughout the recipes you'll see references to Joe's Stuff and dried sliced garlic. Joe's Stuff is a creole seasoning that we use at the New Orleans School of Cooking. It is superb! It's a blend of spices and herbs. The real difference between it and other spice blends is that it only has 2% salt! There's no cayenne in it, the red color is paprika. The dried, sliced garlic has been roasted and freeze dried. It adds a mellow garlic flavor to the dishes plus it's interesting to see in a dish. In addition, you'll see references to the Trinity (onions, bell pepper and celery) and the Pope (fresh garlic). South Louisiana is still predominately Catholic. The French and Spanish kings were Catholic - so that meant everyone had to be Catholic!

So now you have it! Two New Orleans ladies sharing what they know about cooking with children, grandchildren and people from all over the world. Basically, anyone who will listen to us - even in the grocery store line! Enjoy, "pass a good time", and remember to clean your plate. - *Anne & Harriet*

Acknowledgements

Where do we being to say "thank you"? At the beginning of course, with our mothers and grandmothers. They were all wonderful cooks but more importantly, they set good examples of how a mother and grandmother should feed the family.

From Anne, to my husband, Alan, thanks for all the times he's driven me to and from work, folded the clothes, unloaded the dishwasher and in general heard me talk about the book. A special thanks to my sisters, Kathy Medo, Colleen Ryan, Mary Fein and my daughter Beth for recipes and testing of them.

From Harriet, countless friends' and family contributions from recipes to reminders of great times that contributed to the love of those recipes. One of the hardest tasks we faced was narrowing down the recipes to the ninety plus we've chosen to share in this book.

But of all the thanks that we owe to our families, the biggest thanks go to our children and their spouses for giving us our beautiful grandchildren. Hopefully, they will continue the traditions of cooking our New Orleans foods.

Greg and Suzanne Leighton, owners of the New Orleans School of Cooking, planted the idea of a book in our heads and have partnered with us in this project. Jyl Benson was our first contact in explaining to us how it's done. She psyched us up big time! Next, everything was turned over to Jeanne Arceneaux Luna, Director of Marketing at NOSOC. She dove right in and directed us through the entire process.

For countless hours of typing and retyping our recipes and revisions, thanks go to Anne's sister, Mary, Harriet's friend, Melaine Doughty and Marie Miele. Proof reading is an essential part of the process. To that end, thanks to Laurelee Roger Toscano and Jan Leonhard for correcting spelling, punctuation and sentence structure.

Once all the editing and typing was done, the next persons to be involved were our graphic artists, Ali Becnel Solino and Stephen Luna. They managed to give us the look that we envisioned. We wanted to capture the feeling of New Orleans with pictures of the French Quarter. To that end, our photographers, Terry Thibeau, David Boudreaux, Joyce Hanks and Matthew Noel accomplished just that!

Our food stylist, Ann Benoit and her assistant, Thomas F. Dalferes were wonderful to work with. We didn't have a clue how much work was involved in making our food look as good as it tastes. And last but not least, Terry Rayner of Wimmer Press was always there when we needed him. Actually, it was Terry that started the ball rolling when it came to our appearance on QVC. Thank you Terry for a beautiful product and a remarkable experience.

We hope you enjoy cooking our family recipes and reading stories about life in New Orleans. If you bought our book as a souvenir, we hope every time you open the pages, you will reminisce about your experiences here seeing our beautiful architecture, learning the history, and of course, enjoying the fabulous food. We also hope you share some of our recipes with your family and make more memories around your table. Of course most importantly . . .

Laissez les bons temps rouler (let the good times roll)! - *Anne & Harriet*

1

Appetizers

White Cheddar Cheese Dip

I would say that most New Orleanians like to cook. But, for one reason or another, it isn't always possible. Not to worry however, because some of our grocery stores have great catering kitchens!

My son Timothy's wife, Stacey, is not one to buy prepared foods for the most part. She's one of those talented cooks that can taste a dish and pretty much recreate it. One such dish is a dip that's made at our local grocery store. She played with it a little and mastered it. White cheddar cheese dip is easy to make and so delicious. – *Anne*

INGREDIENTS

- 8 oz. white cheddar cheese, chopped
- ⅛ cup mayonnaise to get to a crumbly dip consistency, start with 1/8 cup and add a little at a time until you like the texture
- 1 cup roasted pecans, medium chopped
- 3 toes (cloves) garlic, (about 1 tsp.) pressed in a garlic press
- ½ bunch green onion, finely chopped
  Pinch cayenne (or more to taste)
- ½ tsp. Worcestershire sauce

INSTRUCTIONS

- Place chopped cheese into a food processor.
- Chop on pulse until crumbly.
- Transfer to a large bowl.
- Add remaining ingredients.
- Stir until blended.
- Serve at room temperature with crackers of your choice.

ingredients

½ lb. bacon, slice bacon
    strips in half
24 large dates, remove seeds
24 pecan halves, plain or
    honey roasted

Death on a Toothpick

A big part of life in the French Quarter is about socializing with your neighbors on the "stoop" (front steps) of your house. Even though we are perched in the center of one of the most historic neighborhoods in the world, you will not find a more neighborly, friendly place. Besides, my neighbors were quality people from all over the world. I really enjoyed finding unique recipes to share with everyone on the stoop. This was a favorite of mine. The dates bring an international flavor while the bacon and pecans are Louisiana all the way. They are easy and quick to make, full of flavor and taste! A great reflection of French Quarter life. – Harriet

INSTRUCTIONS

- Preheat oven to 350°.
- In a large skillet over medium high heat, cook bacon until limp. Remove from heat and drain.
- Stuff each date with a pecan half.
- Wrap each date with a strip of bacon and secure with a toothpick.*
  Repeat until all dates are wrapped.
- Line a sheet pan with parchment paper and arrange wrapped dates on the pan. Bake until bacon is crispy and dates are heated through, about 10-12 minutes.
- Remove and drain on a paper towel. Serve warm.

*Soak toothpicks in water to keep them from burning in the oven.

ingredients

½ cup sour cream
1 cup mayonnaise
1½ tbl. curry powder
½ tsp. Joe's Stuff seasoning
1 tbl. Lea & Perrins
(Worcestershire)
1 tsp. Crystal hot sauce
2 tsp. grated onion or
onion juice
3 tbl. ketchup

Dip for Everything

From vegetables to sliced meats and even a po-boy, this dip is fantastic and goes well with anything. I love it. Since my housewife days in the 1970's in Metairie, to my move to the Quarter and back again to the suburbs, this recipe continues to make my life so easy. I think it's a recipe that is simple and quick. And, I consider it culinary ammunition.......make it on Monday and it is still "Wow" on Wednesday.

If you are single, married or a working mother, you can make this ahead and keep in the fridge. Then, easily pack it up and carry it to the office, a PTA meeting or take it next door. Just bring along carrots, celery, cherry tomatoes, broccoli, and cauliflower, washed and cut into bite sized pieces. Whatever you like. And, voilà instant party food! *– Harriet*

INSTRUCTIONS

- In a large mixing bowl combine all ingredients thoroughly and chill at least two hours.

HINT: If you want to add more flavor, just increase the amount of curry powder by ¼ teaspoon until you reach the desired flavor. This is great served with boiled shrimp as a substitute for remoulade sauce or a dip for Buffalo wings.

ingredients

4 doz. oysters and their
    liquid (we call it liquor),
    rough chopped
1 stick butter for sautéing
2 bunches green onions,
    finely chopped
4-6 toes (cloves) garlic, finely
    chopped
6 tbl. all-purpose flour
2 bunches parsley, finely
    chopped
1 cup oyster liquor (if you
    don't have enough, add
    heavy cream to make up
    the difference)
Joe's Stuff seasoning to
    taste
Pinch cayenne
8 Pepperidge Farms patty
    shells

Oyster Patties

An authentic New Orleans holiday table always includes oysters. It's a Thanksgiving and Christmas tradition that my family carries on to this day. My Mama and Nan made oyster patties during the Holidays. After all these years, I'm not ashamed to admit that I preferred Nan's rendition. My children demand that I make them. I'm still waiting for my grandchildren to appreciate them. I know it's just a matter of time! – *Anne*

INSTRUCTIONS

- Preheat oven to 350°.
- Drain oysters well - save oyster liquor, rough chop oysters into bite sized pieces.
- In a small sauce pan, heat oyster liquor on low heat. Strain and set aside.
- In a large skillet on medium high heat, melt butter. Sauté green onions and garlic for four minutes.
- Lower heat to medium and stir in the flour with a whisk. Whisk continuously to blend. Cook roux for about four minutes to create a blonde roux.
- Add the parsley and blend. Gradually add warmed oyster liquor to the roux mixing with a whisk to fully incorporate.
- Bring heat back up to high and add oysters (they will shrink and start to curl up), Joe's Stuff seasoning and cayenne to taste. Stir and continue to heat until mixture thickens, about 5-8 minutes.
- Heat pastry shells on a baking pan. When hot and sauce is a nice thick consistency, ladle the oyster mixture into the pastry shells and serve.

HINT: You can use petite shells and serve as cocktail appetizers. You just follow the same directions but chop the oysters a little smaller. Also, this is delicious served over pasta as an entrée.

ingredients

- 4 whole artichokes (If you're going to do this you might as well make enough for the next day.)
- 1 gal. water for boiling artichokes
- 3-4 medium onions, finely chopped
- 21 toes (cloves) (YES!) garlic, finely chopped
- 2 cups Italian style bread crumbs
- 2¼ cups Parmesan cheese, finely grated
- 2¼ cups Romano cheese, finely grated
- 1 tbl. Kosher salt
- 1 tsp. black pepper
- 1 cup olive oil for drizzling

Stuffed Artichokes

New Orleans has a large population of families with Sicilian heritage. Among many food items they brought to the city was the artichoke. We eat them in a variety of ways: grilled, steamed and stuffed.

Now, here is the honest truth – stuffing artichokes is a "pain in the neck" to make and time consuming. But the results are well worth the effort!

When my children got old enough to help, I would prep the artichokes, prepare the stuffing, put everything in a large salad bowl and set it in the middle of our round dinner table. Everyone would stuff their own. – *Anne*

INSTRUCTIONS

- Prepare the artichokes by cutting off the tips on all leaves. Open up and remove the thistle (fuzzy part in center).
- Cut off a portion of the stem to create a flat bottom.
- Cover with water and boil for 15 minutes. Drain.
- Combine all ingredients (except olive oil) in a large bowl. Mix well.
- Begin stuffing the leaves from the bottom up. Don't be stingy!
- Fill the cavity with the extra filling. After stuffing, hold the artichokes in both hands and compress gently.
- Drizzle olive oil over the artichokes.
- In a pot large enough to steam side by side, add ½ inch of water. Cover, bring to a boil, reduce heat to a simmer. Periodically check the water level. Steam until the leaves pull out easily (about 45 minutes).
- Serve warm, cold or room temperature.

ingredients

1½ doz. hard boiled eggs,
   peeled, cut in half
   lengthwise with yolks
   removed. Set aside.
1½ tsp. Joe's Stuff seasoning
 ½ tsp. white vinegar
  1 tbl. olive oil
  1 tbl. minced parsley
 ½ cup mayonnaise
 ⅛ cup green onion finely
   chopped

Stuffed Eggs

When I lived in the French Quarter, my wonderful neighbors John and John celebrated New Year's Eve with an incredible party where we ate and drank like all devoted "Quarterites" do so well! The funny thing is their New Year's celebration took place in June! So, is their celebration the end of the season or the beginning? Who knew? Who cared? As we all know here in New Orleans, if there isn't a clear reason to celebrate, we just make one up! I looked forward to it every year and must say their stuffed egg recipe was a total hit. Every chance I get, I make this recipe. It is just as perfect for a picnic by the river or a canapé at a fancy Uptown gathering – simply add ingredients to change it up. Good eating. – Harriet

INSTRUCTIONS

- In a mixing bowl, mash yolks thoroughly.
- Mix in remaining ingredients and blend thoroughly.
- Adjust seasoning if necessary.
- Fill each egg half and garnish with green onion.

HINT: You can vary the recipe by adding minced crispy bacon, crumbled blue cheese, or minced chilled seafood. Even a few capers or black olives add a little zippiness to this recipe. Drizzle the eggs with remoulade too. Delicious!

Cheese Rounds

This is a very popular item found on party tables in New Orleans. The taste is exactly like cheese straws but a lot easier to make, I think. Being a Cajun girl, I like a little kick to my food. But if you don't, eliminate the cayenne pepper. But you know what – try it! You're learning a new item – so start off with a small amount of cayenne. You can always add more the next time. – *Anne*

INGREDIENTS

1 stick butter, softened (not melted)

4 cups medium or sharp yellow cheddar cheese, shredded

1 cup all purpose flour

½ tsp. salt

¾ tsp. cayenne pepper

½ cup pecan halves, for decoration

INSTRUCTIONS

- Place all ingredients except pecans into a food processor. Blend until thoroughly mixed and the mixture forms a ball.
- Divide the mixture in half.
- Roll into 2 logs about 2 inches in diameter and wrap in wax paper. Refrigerate until firm, about 1 hour or so. This allows the butter to firm up so that it will be easy to slice the logs. You also don't have to make these the same day.
- Preheat oven to 350°.
- Remove logs from refrigerator, slice thinly, about a smidgen less than ¼ inch and arrange on an ungreased cookie sheet. Gently press a pecan half on each slice for decoration.
- Bake for 10 – 15 minutes until a golden brown. Remove from oven and cool.

HINT: In my opinion, a food processor is essential to make these. It shreds beautifully and then processes the mixture perfectly.

Crabmeat Dip

All New Orleanians have a good crab dip recipe and this is mine. Ms. Doris, mother to my French Quarter neighbor David, is a retired home economics teacher from Orange, Texas. Her recipe archive is bottomless. Our stoops (front steps) would truly light up when Ms. Doris and her husband Junior would come and visit their son. In my heart, I feel that Ms. Doris has the culinary sense of a New Orleanian. I fell in love with this dish the first time David served it. It is the perfect combination of flavors and crab meat. I am so grateful she and David shared this with me. As a New Orleanian, I am programed to love crab. I think it's in my DNA, so a great crab recipe is to be cherished for sure, especially if it's created by dear friends. – *Harriet*

INGREDIENTS

- 1 stick butter
- ¼ cup all-purpose flour
- ¼ cup green onions, chopped and divided
- ¼ cup parsley, chopped and divided
- 2 cups heavy cream
- 1 tbl. cream sherry
- 2 tsp. Joe's Stuff seasoning
- 1 cup Gruyère cheese, shredded
- 1 lb. fresh crabmeat
- 2 tbl. lemon juice

INSTRUCTIONS

- In a large sauté pan over medium heat, melt butter and add the flour. Stir continuously for about 3 minutes.
- Watch carefully so it doesn't brown. You want your roux to be white in color but cooked long enough to get rid of the flour taste.
- Add half of the green onion and parsley and stir. Cook for about 1 minute.
- Slowly whisk in cream, sherry, Joe's Stuff seasoning and cheese.
- Continue to stir while the cheese melts.
- Add the remaining green onion and parsley.
- Add crabmeat and lemon juice, stir and cook for one minute. Adjust seasoning if necessary.
- Remove from heat, transfer to a heat resistant dish and serve warm with crackers.

HINT: This dip is also great chilled.

Artichoke Balls

Throughout this book, you will notice I mention my paternal aunt we called Nan. What a character she was! She had a love for life that couldn't be matched. As she grew older, she would sing in the movie theater, talk loudly, and say whatever was on her mind - certainly not politically correct by today's standards! Now that I'm much older, I completely understand where she was coming from - I've become just like her!

Nan was a terrific cook. Her kitchen was unbelievably small - the only counter space was about 1 foot on each side of the big sink. Whenever there was a function involving food, she was generally asked to bring her famous artichoke balls. One time, she was even featured in our local newspaper, The Times Picayune. - *Anne*

INGREDIENTS

1 (12 oz.) can artichoke hearts in water, drained
1 cup + 3 tbl. Italian style bread crumbs
½ cup + 3 tbl. Romano cheese, finely grated
½ cup + 3 tbl. Parmesan cheese, finely grated
2 eggs, beaten
2 tbl. olive oil
5-8 toes(cloves) garlic, pressed in a garlic press (it depends on how much you like garlic)

INSTRUCTIONS

- Drain artichokes and mash in a food processor.
- To this add 1 cup of bread crumbs, ½ cup of Romano cheese, ½ cup of Parmesan cheese and eggs. Reserve remaining bread crumbs and cheese for coating the artichoke balls. Mix thoroughly.
- Heat olive oil in a large skillet on low heat. Sauté garlic to mellow out the flavor, about 2 minutes, careful not to brown it.
- Add the artichoke mixture to the skillet and continue to cook on low fire for 5 minutes, stirring lightly. This will cook the eggs and bring the flavors together. Remove from fire, cool and refrigerate until the mixture firms up, about 2 hours.
- Combine the remaining breadcrumbs, Parmesan and Romano cheeses in bowl. Shape the chilled artichoke mixture into bite sized balls. Roll in breadcrumb and cheese mixture to lightly coat. Arrange the artichoke balls on a platter. Refrigerate until needed.

Cheese Balls

Cheese balls have always been a "go to" for parties. They're easy to make and so flexible in flavors by simply changing the cheeses. In the 50's, 60's and 70's, we were pretty much limited to Ritz crackers to accompany a cheese ball. Now, with all the different types of crackers available, the possibilities are endless! – *Anne*

INGREDIENTS

- 1 (8 oz.) pkg. Philadelphia Cream Cheese, room temperature
- ½ lb. sharp cheddar cheese (yellow or white) finely grated
- 4 oz. Bleu cheese, room temperature
- 2 toes (cloves) garlic pressed in a garlic press
- ½ cup green onions, finely chopped
- ¼ tsp. Worcestershire sauce
- ⅛ tsp. cayenne pepper
- 1 cup roasted pecans finely chopped – divided if you want 2 smaller balls
- 1 bunch parsley, finely chopped - divided if you want 2 smaller balls

INSTRUCTIONS

- Using a food processor, combine cheeses with all ingredients except the parsley and pecans. Mix until ingredients are thoroughly combined and you have a smooth, creamy texture.
- Place covered in the refrigerator for about 2 hours. Remove and shape into one large ball, the size of a cabbage, or two smaller balls the size of a softball.
- Combine parsley and pecans. Roll the ball in the mixture, place on platter and refrigerate until ready to serve.

HINT: If you want "two for the price of one" roll one ball in roasted pecans and the other in finely chopped parsley.

2

Soups

Oyster Soup

My mother's oyster soup is a staple on the Ryan girls' (my maiden name) Thanksgiving and Christmas dinner tables and a true part of our family food traditions. November and December fall right in the middle of peak oyster season in South Louisiana. You know those months spelled with an "r" signal the cool weather and tides that make for the salty goodness in a South Louisiana oyster.

The secret to making this soup perfectly is to use oyster liquor. The liquor I refer to is the actual liquid that comes from the oyster when it's opened. To get authentic oyster liquor these days, you almost have to commit to actually shucking them yourself. That can be not only time consuming but logistically impossible if you don't live near the coast. Most oysters you buy in the container have been washed and the liquid you get in the container isn't as strong. But at any rate, keep that liquid because it will be key to getting a rich soup. – *Anne*

INGREDIENTS

3 doz. oysters and their liquor
1 stick butter
1 cup onions, finely chopped
2 bunches green onions, finely chopped (reserve some for topping)
4 toes garlic, finely chopped
½ cup all-purpose flour
1 qt. heavy cream
1 qt. half and half
½ bunch parsley, finely chopped
1 tbl. Joe's Stuff seasoning or to taste
Pinch cayenne (optional)

INSTRUCTIONS

• In a soup pot, poach the oysters in their liquor for about 8 minutes or until the oysters begin to plump up. Continuously skim off the scum (I don't know what else to call it) that rises to the top. Discard it. Remove from heat. Using a slotted spoon, remove oysters from liquor and set aside. Keep oyster liquor warm.

• In a large skillet, melt butter over medium heat. Add all onions and sauté five minutes. Do not brown.

• Add garlic and continue to sauté another 2 minutes.

• Reduce heat to low and gradually stir in the flour to make a smooth blonde roux. Cook 4-5 minutes.

• SLOWLY whisk the roux mixture into warm oyster liquor until fully incorporated. Then whisk in cream and half and half.

• Bring to a boil, reduce to a simmer for 10 minutes. Add oysters and simmer for another 5 minutes.

• Add parsley and Joe's Stuff seasoning. Simmer for another 5 minutes. Adjust seasonings. If you want a slight kick, add a pinch of cayenne (I always do, but more than a pinch).

HINT: When serving, sprinkle a few finely chopped green onions for garnish.

INGREDIENTS

6 roasted* red bell peppers, peeled and roughly chopped

1 stick butter

1 small onion, finely chopped

½ cup all-purpose flour

2 cups chicken stock

1 qt. heavy whipping cream

1 tbl. Joe's Stuff seasoning (or more to taste)

Pinch cayenne pepper (or more to taste)

¼ cup cream sherry (optional)

½ bunch parsley, finely chopped

½ bunch green onions, finely chopped

Roasted Red Pepper Soup

New Orleans is a soup city. Bisques with their creamy elegance represent the classical cooking methods embraced by the Creole cooks. The magic of the bisque lies in its flexibility to become transformed with the addition of a few seasonal ingredients. In the spring, when the crabs are at their best, add lump crab meat and Brie cheese. Same for summer vegetables. The combinations are endless and give a great base for the wonderful bounty of fresh vegetables and seafood from right here in New Orleans.

This is lovely bisque that is beautiful to look at as well as delicious to eat. By changing the vegetable you can have an entirely different soup. *– Anne*

INSTRUCTIONS

- Melt butter in a skillet over medium fire. Sauté onion until transparent.
- Sprinkle flour over the onions. Reduce heat to low and whisk for 4 minutes (you're making a roux).
- Place all ingredients (EXCEPT parsley and green onions) into a stock pot. Bring to a slight boil, reduce heat and simmer for 15 minutes. If the liquid is getting too thick, add some whole milk.
- Purée the mixture with an immersion blender. If you don't have one, then by all means get one. It's much more efficient than using a blender.
- After blending, add parsley, adjust seasoning if needed.
- When serving sprinkle with green onions.

*You absolutely, positively have to burn the peppers until they are blistered. Place in a zip-lock bag to sweat. Lastly, pick all the burned pepper skin off.

ingredients

1⅓ cup oil (We use lard.) divided into 1/3 cup and 1 cup amounts

4 cups onion, finely chopped

2 cups green bell pepper, finely chopped

2 cups celery, finely chopped

2 tbl. garlic, finely chopped

2 tbl. dried, roasted garlic (optional)

12 cups regular strength chicken stock (We use Minor's or Better Than Bouillon, just follow the directions.)

1 cup all-purpose flour

1½ lbs. sliced andouille sausage, thinly sliced

2 bay leaves

¼ cup Joe's Stuff seasoning to taste (Start off with at least 1/4 cup, you can always add more.)

½ rotisserie chicken, meat pulled from bones and cut into small chunks.

2 cups green onions, finely chopped, for garnish cooked rice if used as an entrée

Chicken & Sausage Gumbo

For native New Orleanians, eating gumbo is a way of life. When I was growing up, the only gumbo we had was seafood gumbo. Then, in the 1970s, a Cajun chef named Paul Prudhomme came to town. Cajun food took the city by storm from that point on.

The Cajuns came to Louisiana in the 1760's after having been exiled from Nova Scotia, Canada. They were settled by the Spanish in southwest Louisiana where they remained pretty much undisturbed until after WWI. Oil and gas were discovered in the 20's and 30's. When that happened they left the prairies and swamps to work in the oil fields. Harriet and I are proud to say we have Cajun Roots. – *Anne & Harriet*

INSTRUCTIONS

- In a soup pot melt ⅓ cup of lard on a high heat.
- Sauté the trinity until well browned. Add the garlic and sauté 2 minutes longer. Add the sausage, mix and set aside.
- In a skillet, melt the remaining lard on medium heat until it begins to simmer. Add the flour and begin whisking the entire time – you're making a dark roux*.
- When brown (color of peanut butter) pour carefully over trinity, etc. mixture.
- Add hot chicken stock, bring to a boil, reduce heat a little (just a few bubbles). Cook for 40 minutes.
- Add chicken right before serving. Skim excess grease and adjust seasoning if needed.
- When serving, sprinkle green onions atop.
- Can be served with or without rice.

*See Lagniappe section for making a roux.

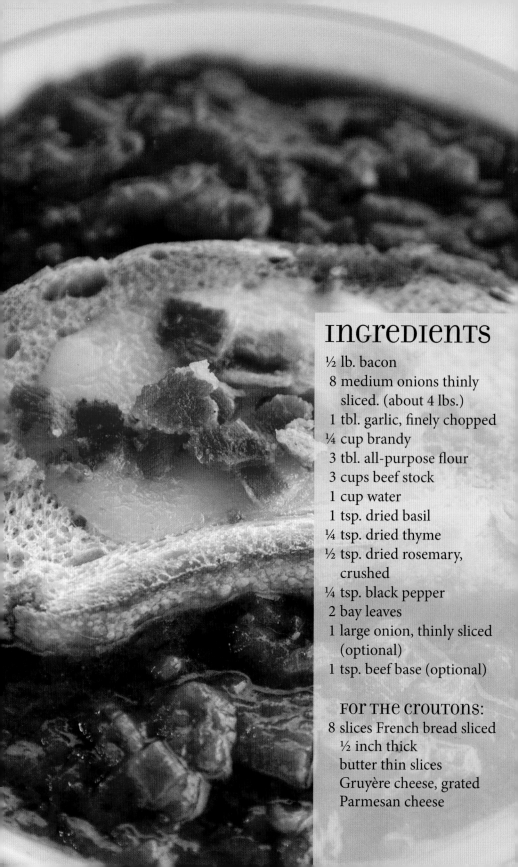

ingredients

½ lb. bacon
8 medium onions thinly
 sliced. (about 4 lbs.)
1 tbl. garlic, finely chopped
¼ cup brandy
3 tbl. all-purpose flour
3 cups beef stock
1 cup water
1 tsp. dried basil
¼ tsp. dried thyme
½ tsp. dried rosemary,
 crushed
¼ tsp. black pepper
2 bay leaves
1 large onion, thinly sliced
 (optional)
1 tsp. beef base (optional)

for the croutons:
8 slices French bread sliced
 ½ inch thick
 butter thin slices
 Gruyère cheese, grated
 Parmesan cheese

French Onion Soup

This is a time consuming recipe but well worth it. The secret to making it is to brown a lot of onions and to have a good beef base. I use Minor's Beef Base or Better Than Bouillon (follow the directions on the jar). - *Anne*

INSTRUCTIONS

- In a 4 qt. Dutch oven, fry off the bacon until crisp. Remove, drain, chop. Set aside for croutons.
- Begin sautéing the onions on high heat until they cook down to a beautiful shade of brown. Toward the end you'll need to lower the fire because the sugar in the onions will begin to stick a little. Work it off.
- Add 1 tbl. of garlic and cook 2 minutes longer.
- Deglaze the pan with brandy, scraping the bits and pieces off the bottom of the pot.
- To give the soup a little body, sprinkle flour over the onions. Lower the fire and cook 4 minutes. By this time you will have a big blob of onions.
- Add the hot beef stock, herbs and seasonings. Bring to a gentle boil then simmer 1 hour. If you think you need a richer flavor add a smidgen of beef base.

CROUTONS:

- Toast the bread on one side under the broiler. Butter the other side, put a slice of Gruyère cheese on it and sprinkle with Parmesan cheese.
- Run under the broiler to melt the cheese.
- Sprinkle the crumbled bacon on the crouton while the cheese is bubbling.

INGReDIeNTS

¼ cup vegetable oil
¼ cup all-purpose flour or gluten free flour
2 cups onion, finely chopped
1 cup celery, finely chopped
½ cup green bell pepper, finely chopped
2 tbl. garlic, finely chopped or use garlic press
½ cup parsley, finely chopped
½ cup green onion, finely chopped (green & white part)
1 large Portobello mushroom, cubed
2 bay leaves
1 tsp. each dried thyme leaves and dried oregano
¼ tsp. cayenne pepper to taste
1 tbl. Joe's Stuff seasoning or more to taste
6 cups mushroom stock*
2 lb. chopped mixed greens (kale, spinach, lettuce, collard, mustard, cabbage)**

Gumbo z'Herbes

You have to have a good Louisiana recipe for gumbo in your back pocket. And, our gumbo ingredients are all about the flavors you get from the spices, the roux, the meats, the Trinity, garlic and the seafood. With that being said, some people can't have gluten found in the flour to make the roux. Some people are vegetarians or simply have a seafood allergy. This gumbo is perfect for anyone who has an issue with certain types of food. And, yet, it still is authentic and full of flavor. I like to change it up sometimes by adding cooked red beans, sweet potatoes and okra. Your favorite seasonal vegetables will work too. Traditionally, we serve Gumbo z'herbes on Good Friday during Lent. - *Harriet*

INSTRUCTIONS

- Begin by making a peanut colored roux*** with the oil and flour on a medium fire.
- The roux should take less than 10 minutes.
- When the roux is the color of dark peanut butter, add the Trinity (onion, celery, bell pepper) and cook together until the onion is transparent.
- Add the garlic and half the parsley, green onion and Portobello mushrooms
- Add the bay leaves, thyme, oregano, cayenne pepper and Joe's Stuff seasoning.
- Sauté a minute or two longer.
- Stir in hot stock.
- Add greens and simmer for 45 minutes, taste for seasoning.
- Garnish with rest of chopped parsley and green onions.

*I used "Better than Bouillon Mushroom Base" Gluten Free.

** Today, in the produce department, there are a variety of salad blends. I selected an assortment of greens that had been cleaned and put in a clear plastic container. Use them. It saves a lot of time. How easy was that?

***See lagniappe on how to make a roux.

This gumbo does not look great, but it is delicious. It's also is gluten free and vegan friendly.

ingredients

6 tbl. vegetable oil

2 lb. sliced okra (I use frozen. It saves a lot of time.)

2 cups onion, finely chopped

1 cup celery, finely chopped

1 cup bell pepper, finely chopped

6 toes garlic (about 2 tbl.), finely chopped

¼ cup sliced dehydrated roasted garlic (optional)

1 (28 oz) can diced tomatoes, drain and save juices

10 cups seafood stock or chicken stock

1 bunch parsley, finely chopped

3 bay leaves

2 tbl. Joe's Stuff seasoning (or more to taste)

1 tsp. salt if needed

⅛ tsp. cayenne (or more to taste)

3 lb. raw shrimp, completely peeled

1 lb. claw crab meat (canned is fine) optional

4-5 cups cooked white rice

1 cup green onions, finely chopped for garnish

Seafood Gumbo

If you're a native of New Orleans or South Louisiana for that matter, born before 1970, then you grew up with Seafood Gumbo, probably on Fridays. New Orleans and South Louisiana are predominately Catholic. Up until the 80's Catholics weren't allowed to eat meat on Friday. We never figured out what a sacrifice it was eating seafood! We just didn't tell the Pope! So, on many Fridays our family would have seafood gumbo.

Okra is a mainstay of Seafood Gumbo. Originally, it was brought to Louisiana by the Africans from the Senegal and Gambia regions. In fact, the Senegal word for okra is quingombo! – *Anne*

INSTRUCTIONS

As much as I use my cast iron pots, I don't use them for this recipe. The cast iron tends to discolor the okra. I use my Le Creuset on top of the stove.

- Heat oil in a stockpot on high heat. Add the okra. Cook down about 20 minutes. As it starts to stick to the pot, lower the fire a little.
- Add the Trinity and sauté for about 20 minutes on medium heat. You might need to add additional oil. Add the garlic, cook 2 minutes more.
- Add the drained tomatoes. Cook down another 15 minutes. Then, add all the liquids and seasonings, EXCEPT the green onions.
- Bring to a boil, reduce heat to a simmer. Cook 1½ hours.
- Return to boil, add shrimp. Cook 8 minutes. You may need to adjust the seasoning, particularly the salt. If using crab meat, add it at the very end just to heat up.

HINT: Seafood gumbo is usually served with rice.

ingredients

1 lb. ground chuck
2 (15 oz.) cans red or
  kidney beans (do not
  drain)
2 (10 oz.) cans Rotel
  tomatoes (do not drain)
2 (4 oz.) cans chopped
  mild green chilies (do not
  drain)
2 (15 oz.) cans tomato
  sauce
2 cups frozen or fresh corn
2 (1.5 oz.) pkg. taco
  seasoning mix

Taco Soup

While visiting my youngest son, Peter, who was attending the College of Santa Fe, I discovered this recipe. One of the great things about Santa Fe is that it is similar to New Orleans in that the culture and the food are so unique. I made it and everyone loved it. Not long after, a version appeared in the Times Picayune. See, great minds think alike! I think it was around the late 80's or early 90's when America was discovering Louisiana food styles as well as Southwestern cuisine. I make this during Mardi Gras. It's great for tailgating and even for college kids cooking in the dorm. You make it in one pot and dip out of it all day long. - *Harriet*

INSTRUCTIONS

- Brown ground meat in a Dutch oven, breaking up the meat while it is browning. When meat is no longer pink, drain.
- Add all of the ingredients and stir to blend.
- Bring to a boil, simmer for 45 min.
- Serve the soup with your favorite toppings.

TOPPING BAR SUGGESTIONS:

1 cup chopped seeded tomatoes
1 cup green onion, finely chopped
½ cup cilantro, finely chopped
½ cup jalapeño pepper, finely chopped, no seeds
½ cup black olives, sliced
1½ cups shredded Mexican cheese blend
Tortilla chips

ST. CHARLES   07

945

3

Salads

Cauliflower with Spinach Dressing

When Alan and I married in 1964 we lived in Springfield, MO where he was a professor. When I look back at those early years I think about how overwhelmed I must have been - newly married, away from home, an additional year to graduate, and then became pregnant right away! Plus, I didn't know how to cook! You can live on scrambled eggs, grilled cheese sandwiches, gumbo, hamburgers and LOVE for only so long!

So I began to peruse magazines from the grocery store trying to diversify my repertoire. I think Family Circle and Good Housekeeping were my favorites. One day, I remember seeing a picture of a magnificent salad in an unusual shaped bowl. We had received one for a wedding present, but needless to say I didn't know what it was for. But then, the light bulb went off and I began to make my first salad! It has been 52 years since that "awakening" and I have been making it ever since. It's pretty to look at, easy to make and delicious. I know you'll enjoy it. – *Anne*

INGREDIENTS

- 1 small head cauliflower, raw
- 1 lb. bacon, well cooked and crumbled
- ¼-½ cup Bleu Cheese, crumbled
- 1 small head lettuce of your choice. (I like Bibb)
- 1 small red onion, sliced very thinly

DRESSING:
- 6 tbl. olive oil
- juice ½ lemon
- 1 tsp. salt
- 1 tsp. pepper
- ½ tsp. granulated sugar
- 4 cups parsley, finely chopped
- 2 toes (cloves) garlic, use a garlic press
- ½ bag fresh spinach, finely chopped

INSTRUCTIONS

- Break cauliflower florets apart.
- Combine bacon, cauliflower and Bleu Cheese
- Tear lettuce into bite-sized pieces.
- Assemble salad in layers: lettuce, cauliflower mixture, red onion. Repeat.
- When ready to serve, pour dressing over salad and toss.

DRESSING:
- Prepare dressing in advance. Place all ingredients in a blender and puree.
- Adjust seasoning if necessary.
- Refrigerate.

INGREDIENTS
4 cups broccoli florets
½ medium red or sweet
  onion, thinly sliced
½ cup golden raisins
¼ cup roasted nuts or seeds
  (pecans, walnuts, pine
  nuts, pumpkin seeds or
  sunflower seeds)
½ cup goat cheese,
  crumbled

DRESSING:
1 cup mayonnaise
2½ tbl. granulated sugar
2 tbl. pear or raspberry
  vinegar

Broccoli Salad

In the 90's, as America became immersed in the Food Channel and cooking, the powers to be at work decided our culinary team at the hospital should spend some time with a professional chef so that we could add a little spark and sizzle to our recipes. I loved it. We learned so much.

Working in a hospital in this area, the expectations were high. Local New Orleans recipes were always used. New Orleanians are a tough audience when it comes to food. Good food, made the Louisiana and New Orleans way, is the expectation. How do we make that happen on a large scale? We certainly had our work cut out for us.

This salad is all about the dressing. – *Harriet*

INSTRUCTIONS

- Cook broccoli for 3-5 minutes in salted water until it is bright but still crisp and tender.
- Drain in a colander, spray with cold water.
- Lay broccoli on a cookie sheet lined with a paper towel or a clean dish towel to dry.
- When dry and cool, place in a salad bowl and combine with sliced onion, raisins, nuts, and goat cheese.
- Make dressing by combining mayonnaise, sugar and vinegar.
- Stir until sugar dissolves. Pour over broccoli and toss to coat.
- Refrigerate for 2 hours and serve.

INGREDIENTS

2 cups whole kernel corn,
  fresh or frozen
1 small red bell pepper,
  finely chopped
1 small green bell pepper,
  finely chopped
1 small sweet red onion,
  finely chopped
1 (15 oz.) can garbanzo
  beans, drained*
1 (4 oz.) can black olives
  sliced or if small enough,
  leave whole
½ bag small frozen green
  peas or edamame, thawed
1 (15 oz.) can black beans,
  washed and drained*
½ cup cilantro, finely
  chopped

DRESSING:

½ cup olive oil
⅓ cup vinegar
½ tsp. garlic powder
½ tsp. fresh ground pepper
 1 tsp. salt
⅛ tsp. cayenne pepper
½ tsp. oregano
½ tsp. cumin
 1 tsp. light brown sugar
2 avocados, sliced for
  garnish

Mardi Gras Salad

My daughter Suzanne and her husband Jim host a New Year's Day gathering every year. It's tradition. Friends, family and plenty of children gather to celebrate. Suzanne always makes this salad. I cook the smothered Cabbage and Black Eyed Peas. Center stage is her salad.

Anne and I do a cooking demonstration once a month for one of our local television stations. We're called the "NOLA Grannies". Recently, we prepared this black bean and corn salad dish. It was an instant hit! The crew suggested we should rename it "Mardi Gras Salad" since we were in the midst of Carnival season. - *Harriet*

INSTRUCTIONS

- Combine all ingredients in a large bowl. Mix thoroughly.
- Place all ingredients except avocados in a bowl and whisk to combine.
- Pour over salad and refrigerate for at least 3 hours.
- Add avocado for garnish. Serve and enjoy.

*When using canned beans, shake the can and listen for the beans moving as that indicates the beans are whole and not mush.

HINT: The addition of sweet potatoes to this recipe adds a fall feeling to this dish. Peel two small sweet potatoes, dice and boil until tender, about 20 minutes. Toss into the salad before you add the dressing. It's lovely.

INGREDIENTS

1 (16 oz.) can whole green
  beans, drained
1 (17 oz.) can tiny green
  peas (I use Dubon)
1 (2 oz.) jar pimento,
  drained
2 small onions (1 red, 1
  white) thinly sliced
½ bell pepper, red or green,
  thinly sliced
5 stalks celery, chopped
  finely
Lettuce of your choice

DRESSING:

¾ cup sugar
 1 cup red wine vinegar
½ cup olive oil

Green Bean Salad

Nan's green bean salad was part of summer. It just wasn't a BBQ without this dish. My husband, Alan, loves this recipe and prepares it all the time.

Plan ahead and make sure to marinate the salad overnight otherwise the flavors will not have a chance to "come together." I prepare using Bibb lettuce but you can use any lettuce of your choice. Steer away from iceberg. It just doesn't bring anything to this recipe. – Anne

INSTRUCTIONS

- Place all drained vegetables in a casserole.
- Pour dressing over everything except lettuce.
- Cover and marinate overnight.
- Before serving the next day, drain well and serve over lettuce.
- Serve cold.

Italian Olive Salad

When the Sicilians came to New Orleans (1890s-1910s) they eventually began to import their olives and olive oils from the old country. Gradually, all kinds of foodstuffs filled the grocery store shelves.

When my grandparents were growing up as well as my parents, there were small Mama and Papa grocery stores on practically every other block of the Quarter. The lower French Quarter was virtually called Little Sicily or Little Palermo. Every Italian restaurant in New Orleans will have an olive salad on the menu. Some are very involved, some quite basic. They were made from very simple ingredients that all Italians had in their pantries and ice boxes.

This is Robert, my husband's brother and his wife, Carolyn's delicious recipe.
- *Anne*

INGREDIENTS

- 1 jar (5.75 oz.) of drained green olives—no seeds—stuffed with pimentos
- ⅔ cup celery, finely chopped
- 3 toes (cloves) garlic, finely chopped
- ¼ cup parsley, finely chopped
- ¾ cup of a good virgin olive oil
- 1 thin slice of lemon cut into 3 triangles

INSTRUCTIONS

- Drain the olives and cut into slices.
- Combine everything in a container and allow to marinate for 4-5 days. It can be served over a leaf of lettuce or made into a sandwich, called a Muffuletta.*

*See Lagniappe for the recipe of the Mufffuletta.

Mixed Greens with Robin Family Pepper Jelly Dressing

This dressing is a great way to use the Robin Pepper Jelly to add spunk and flavor to salads. You'll find the main recipe for the Robin Family Pepper Jelly in the Lagniappe section - *Harriet*

INGREDIENTS

- 1 pkg. assorted mix baby greens and lettuce
- 1 tbl. sun dried tomatoes, slivered
- ½ cup pecans or pine nuts, toasted
- ½ cup golden raisins
- ½ cup goat cheese or cheese of your choice, crumbled
- ½ cup pitted Kalamata olives, drained
- ½ cup croutons
- 1 cup sliced strawberries, fresh

DRESSING:
- ¼ cup Robin Family Pepper Jelly*
- 1 tbl. vinegar of choice
- ½ tsp. garlic powder
- ½ tsp. kosher salt
- ½ cup extra virgin olive oil

INSTRUCTIONS

- Mix all ingredients together in a salad bowl.

DRESSING:
- Combine all dressing ingredients in a small jar shake well. When adding dressing to salad greens just lightly coat the leaves with dressing.

HINT: You can add some blackberry preserves to the vinaigrette, and baste a pork tenderloin with it too. Simple and fantastic.

*See Lagniappe section for recipe.

4

Meat Entrées

Flank Steak

We never had flank steak growing up - it wasn't popular. But in the 80's, it came of age and now we have it all the time. This recipe was given to me by my sister Kathy. She claims not to be a good cook but she is. She'll try a lot of recipes, whereas I'm usually content to do the same old thing over and over again. Flank steak needs to be marinated. *- Anne*

INGREDIENTS

- ⅔ cup soy sauce
- 3 tbl. dried minced onion
- 3 toes (cloves) garlic, pressed
- ⅔ cup olive oil
- 6 tbl. red wine vinegar (Balsamic would be great, also)
- 1 flank steak

INSTRUCTIONS

THE MARINADE:

- In a mixing bowl, whisk ingredients together. Place steak in a gallon sized Ziplock bag, pour in marinade and seal tightly. Place in the refrigerator and marinate for a minimum of 8 hours.

TO COOK FLANK STEAK:

- Remove steak from marinating bag and place under a broiler on baking sheet or place directly on the grill to cook to desired doneness. Transfer liquid marinade to sauce pan and bring to a boil. Reduce by a third for about 5 minutes and use it as a basting sauce.

HINT: When slicing the flank steak always slice against the grain on a slight diagonal. Any left overs are great the next day for enchiladas.

ingredients

2½-3 lbs. chicken cut up, or
    buy the pieces you enjoy
    eating. Run under cold
    water and pat dry.
  3 tbl. or more divided in
    half Joe's Stuff seasoning
  ½ cup vegetable oil, divided
  ½ cup + 2 tbl. flour
  2 cups onions, finely
    chopped
  1 cup celery, finely chopped
  ½ cup bell pepper, finely
    chopped
  ½ cup parsley, finely
    chopped
  ½ cup green onions, finely
    chopped
3-4 toes (cloves) garlic, finely
    chopped or use garlic
    press
1-2 bay leaves
  1 (15 oz.) can tomato sauce
  2 cups chicken stock*
  ½ cup white vermouth

Chicken in Gravy

One of my favorite childhood meals was chicken in red gravy or in brown gravy for Sunday lunch. I remember it with peas and corn in the gravy. Yes, my mother and grandmother would add all the leftovers to the gravy adding flavor and color. It was so good that I always wanted seconds. – *Harriet*

INSTRUCTIONS

- Season chicken on both sides with ½ of the Joe's Stuff seasoning.
- Heat an empty Dutch oven on a medium fire for about 4 minutes.
- Add 2 tbl. vegetable oil to hot pot.
- When the oil is shimmering, brown chicken on all sides. Remove from pot and set aside.
- Now is the time to make your roux. Over medium heat add ½ cup flour to the remaining vegetable oil in the hot pot.
- As you stir the roux, make sure to scrape all the fond (bits of chicken and seasoning) off the bottom of the pot.
- Continue to stir and cook the roux to a good peanut butter color.
- Be careful not to burn the roux (STIR, STIR). At this point, add the Trinity (onion, celery, bell pepper). Stir to blend.
- Cook roux and vegetables together until the onions are transparent.
- Now add the chopped garlic, parsley, green onions, and Joe's Stuff seasoning to taste. Continue to cook for a minute or two.
- Add bay leaves, tomato sauce, and hot chicken stock.*
- Wash the sauce can out with the white vermouth or a little stock.
- Put chicken and the juice from the chicken back into the pot.
- Cover and simmer until chicken is cooked and tender, falling off the bone tender. About 1 to 1½ hours.
- Taste and adjust seasoning.

*If you have fresh homemade chicken stock on hand, use it. I use chicken base and water or ready made stock for this dish.

ingredients

4 tbl. vegetable oil
3 lb. chuck roast
6 toes (cloves) garlic, divided
  into 2 portions
3 tbl. Joe's Stuff seasoning
¼ cup all-purpose flour
2 cups onions, finely chopped
1 cup celery, finely chopped
½ cup green, red, orange or
  yellow bell pepper, finely
  chopped
1 cup parsley, finely chopped
  and divided in half
1 cup green onions, finely
  chopped and divided in half
1 (15 oz.) can tomato sauce
3 cups chicken stock*
1 lb. spaghetti
  A little butter and olive oil
  to toss in cooked spaghetti

Daube & Spaghetti

Daube is a real Creole dish. Anne and I were so proud to appear on the Steve Harvey show and share this classic New Orleans recipe with his audience. It was a hit. Daube and spaghetti is the dinner of choice for all my family members when it's time to celebrate birthdays or special occasions. They always ask Momma to cook it! My daughter Victoria always asks me to make this for her birthday dinner. And, I love doing that for her, all my kids and grandchildren. I think I've cooked it hundreds of times over the last 50 years. And, I just love it every time. Basically, it is meat in a reddish brown gravy served over spaghetti. But, it doesn't have to be Italian. You can serve the daube over rice, mashed potatoes or whatever you prefer. Even slice it up and make a po-boy sandwich with the gravy. *- Harriet*

INSTRUCTIONS

- Heat a Dutch oven on the stove using medium high heat for 3-5 minutes.
- Add vegetable oil to heated pot.
- Stuff chuck roast with 3 toes of garlic (which have been cut in half) by making slits in the meat and pushing the garlic in, go all around the meat doing this until 3 toes of garlic are used.
- Season meat all over with Joe's Stuff Seasoning.
- Put roast in hot pot and brown on all sides. When the pot releases the meat (about 3-4 minutes) on one side, turn over and brown the opposite side.
- When the roast is brown on both sides, remove from pot and put aside.
- Keep the pot on medium heat.
- Sprinkle flour over the oil and begin your roux. You may have to add a little more oil to make a smooth roux.
- Do not leave your roux, continue to stir constantly and scrape up all the brown bits (fond) on the bottom of the pot.
- When the roux is color of dark peanut butter, add the Trinity (onion, celery and bell pepper). Cook until onions are soft, about 5-7 minutes.
- To this, add the garlic, green onion and parsley and 1 tablespoon of Joe's Stuff seasoning. Continue to cook for about 2 minutes.
- Add tomato sauce and 2 cups of chicken stock.
- Stir to blend. If too thick, add more chicken stock.
- Return meat to the pot, cover and simmer for 2-3 hours until meat is tender.
- Cook spaghetti according to package directions. Drain and add a little olive oil and butter to keep spaghetti separated.

*I use Minor's Chicken Base, Better Than Bouillon or boxed stock.

INGREDIENTS

4 lb. fryer chicken cut into pieces (have the breasts cut into 4 pieces)

3 tbl. Joe's Stuff seasoning

3 tbl. vegetable oil

40 toes (cloves) garlic, peeled

½ cup cream sherry divided into two portions

1 tbl. fresh rosemary, minced

1 tbl. fresh thyme, minced
Zest 1 lemon

1 cup regular strength chicken stock

½ stick butter, cut into little pats

1 bunch parsley, finely chopped

Forty Toes of Garlic Chicken

Sounds outrageous, doesn't it - but it is delicious! The garlic roasts and becomes very mild. It makes a beautiful gravy which we pour over rice, noodles or mashed potatoes. - *Anne*

INSTRUCTIONS

- Preheat oven to 400°.
- Generously season chicken with Joe's Stuff seasoning.
- Heat oil in a Dutch oven over a medium high heat. Brown the chicken. Remove and set aside.
- Lower the temperature to medium and add the garlic to the drippings. While you're lightly browning the garlic, scrape the drippings (fond) off. When the garlic is golden brown remove from pot. Set aside.
- Pour in 1/4 cup of sherry to deglaze the pan juices. It will sizzle.
- Place everything into the pot EXCEPT the chicken stock, parsley and butter.
- Bake covered for 30 minutes. Remove from oven and turn pieces over. Return to oven.
- Continue baking another 20 minutes or until the chicken is cooked and fork tender.
- Remove to a platter.
- Return the pot back to the stove and mash the garlic.
- Add the remaining sherry and cook about 3 minutes on a medium fire.
- Next, add the chicken stock and cook for 5 minutes.
- Turn the fire off. Now you're going to "cream the gravy". Finish off the gravy by putting butter, 1 pat at a time, into the gravy. As one pat is almost completely melted, add another stirring the entire time.
- Finally, add the parsley.

HINT: Serve over rice, noodles or mashed potatoes.

INGREDIENTS

¾ cup stale French bread, soaked in milk or water and squeezed dry

1 lb. ground chuck (I use an 80/20 mix)

½ lb. raw Italian Sausage, removed from its casing

¾ cup Parmesan cheese, grated

7 toes (cloves) garlic, pressed

3 eggs, beaten

1 bunch parsley, finely chopped

1 cup onion, finely chopped

1 tsp. salt

1 tsp. pepper

Olive oil for browning the meatballs

Meatballs

Nan made the best meatballs in the family. They were always so light and flavorful. Years ago at the Cooking School we used to make these for the "Hands On" classes. The School's recipe included chopped onions, which I had never experienced in meatballs before. It was a wonderful addition. Then when Harriet and I appeared on "The Steve Harvey Show" the first time, we made Meatballs and Spaghetti. Harriet said she always included raw Italian sausage in her meatball mixture. I tried it - another terrific addition!

This recipe makes a lot so freeze some. If you make Gayle's Red Gravy* recipe and freeze her gravy in portions, you'll have a lot of servings on hand. - *Anne*

INSTRUCTIONS

- Combine all ingredients (EXCEPT olive oil). Work together by hand – do not overwork. The mixture will be soft. Shape into small balls – about the size of a golf ball.
- Brown (not cook) the meatballs either in a skillet in olive oil, or in the oven, otherwise they'll fall apart in the gravy. Save any drippings to add to the red gravy.
- When the red gravy is almost finished cooking, you'll need to add the uncooked meatballs. Cook for 30 minutes.

*See Lagniappe for Red Gravy recipe.

Paneé Meat 1

We know it seems strange to include 2 recipes of the same dish - BUT - we're doing it anyway! Paneé meat has special memories for the both of us. We couldn't decide which to use, so you're getting both!

This is an all-time favorite of my childhood, my children's childhood, and now a favorite of my grandchildren. Paneé in French means pan fry. The meat is battered and fried in a skillet. My family battered in cracker crumbs crushed with a rolling pin.

When my youngest son Timothy and his family come home for the holidays, he always wants to have paneé meat. The whole family gathers. It's a big production with 11 people eating who have hearty appetites. So we do it assembly line: Timothy, Abby (my granddaughter) and me. It's a lot of work, but it's fun. The hardest part is keeping the troops from eating the meat as we cook it! – Anne

INGREDIENTS

2 sleeves Saltines or unsalted crackers (about 80 crackers)

8 veal rounds (cutlets)

¼ cup Joe's Stuff seasoning or more if needed

1 cup whole milk

2 large eggs

1 cup peanut oil

INSTRUCTIONS

- Crush the crackers, not too fine, but not huge chunks either.
- Trim the meat into portion sizes.
- Pound the meat and generously season it.
- Prepare an egg wash. Dip the meat in the egg wash then in the cracker crumbs. Press the crumbs in. Don't stack the breaded meats on top of each other.
- Heat the oil in a deep, skillet on a medium – high fire.
- When frying the meat don't overload the skillet. Fry about 2-3 minutes on each side – should be a beautiful medium brown.
- Drain on paper towel. Sometimes we'll sprinkle grated Parmesan cheese on top.

Paneé Meat 2

You often hear New Orleanians talk about their mother's paneé meat recipe. We all grew up with paneé meat for dinner. Really, you can paneé anything. What's paneé? It's simply the cooking term for sautéing meat with a light breading in a small amount of oil. It's not deep frying at all. It's quick because you pound out your meat thinly. You paneé cutlets one after another in a pretty quick pace.

My mother always made paneé meat at least once a week. She served it with green noodles, corn and a salad of tomato and asparagus. I still do the same. It's my son Michael's favorite dish. And, if he is around while I'm cooking this dish, he can eat the cutlets as fast as I can paneé them. It makes me smile to think about it. – *Harriet*

INGREDIENTS

- 2 cups bread crumbs
- ½ cup Parmesan cheese, grated
- 1 tsp. dried rosemary, crushed
- 1 tsp. dried oregano
- 1 tsp. dried basil
  Joe's Stuff seasoning to taste
- ¾ cup olive oil, divided
- 7 pieces (cutlets) beef, veal, chicken or pork

INSTRUCTIONS

- In a shallow pan or plate, make a seasoned breading by combining bread crumbs with the cheese, rosemary, oregano and basil.
- Pound the cutlets fairly thin.
- Prepare each cutlets by brushing lightly with olive oil and season with Joe's Stuff seasoning.
- In a large skillet, heat a portion of olive oil over medium high heat.
- When olive oil is heated, coat the cutlets in the breading and place in pan. Fill the pan but be careful not to overcrowd. You can cook this amount in 3-4 batches. You might have to add a little more olive oil.
- Cook on each side for 2 minutes. Remove and drain.

ingredients

3 lb. chuck roast
2 tsp. salt
3 tsp. Joe's Stuff seasoning
3 toes garlic, sliced into
  thirds
¼ cup vegetable oil
12 small baby or Yukon
  Gold potatoes
1-2 onions, peeled and
  quartered
3 whole carrots, peeled and
  cut into thirds
2 whole celery stalks, cut
  into thirds
2 cups chicken or beef
  stock

Pot of Roast Beef

My roast beef is so good. Ask my kids. And, after earning grandmother rights, I can say that. It's All-American. You can put all the vegetables you want together with the meat. Your choice. If you work outside the home, this is a wonderful crock-pot, slow cook recipe. If you are at home on a Saturday, you can cook it all day long in the oven. Of course, leftovers can be used for sandwiches and to top a salad too. – *Harriet*

INSTRUCTIONS

- Rinse roast and pat dry.
- Prepare the roast by making nine small slits evenly dispersed in the roast. Stuff each slit with a piece of garlic.
- Season entire roast with salt and Joe's Stuff seasoning.
- In a large Dutch oven, heat oil over medium high heat. Brown roast on all sides.
- Add vegetables and stock. Stock should come up to ½ of the roast.
- Bring to a boil, reduce to a simmer and cover with a tight fitting lid. Cook for 2½ - 3 hours, checking often to make sure the stock has not fully evaporated. If necessary, add more stock.
- When roast is cooked through and vegetables are tender, remove from heat and serve family style on a platter.

HINT: You can add any type of vegetables to this recipe. Carrots, celery, peas, and corn are all excellent and add color and flavor. You can even add a bit of red wine to the stock. It adds a little bit of zing. If using a crock pot, reduce stock by ½ cup because the crock pot will create more liquid.

INGREDIENTS

1 lb. red beans, soaked
   overnight to soften
10 cups water
2 tbl. bacon fat (lard)
3 cups onion, finely
   chopped
1½ cups celery, finely
   chopped
¾ cup green bell pepper,
   finely chopped
1 tsp. thyme
2-3 bay leaves
4 toes (cloves) garlic, finely
   chopped
2 tbl. Joe's Stuff seasoning
2-3 tbl. chicken or ham base
1 lb. smoked ham hock
½ cup parsley
½ cup green onions, finely
   chopped

Red Beans & Rice

In New Orleans, red beans are a Monday classic. My Mother really did do the wash on Monday. It was an all day affair for her. She played the soap operas on our floor model radio. While she cooked, washed and ironed, the background sounds of the heart wrenching stories and adventures of Stella Dallas and others filled the house. And, the whole while I'm sure she prayed that it wouldn't rain. Heaven forbid if it rained. The mad scramble began - Momma pulling the clothes off the line and I would be behind her picking up the socks and undies that fell to the ground. Clothes pins flying and baskets piled high meant the entire house was covered with the fresh starched dresses, skirts and more. A lot of work. That really does explain why this dish is so important to the Monday culture. You can leave it and go. Also, no matter if you were rich or poor, uptown or downtown, we all were eating red beans on Monday. Red beans, the classic way, cooked all day is one of the best dishes of New Orleans and truly ties us together.
– Harriet

INSTRUCTIONS

- In a large stock pot, add soaked beans and water. The water level should be at least one inch over beans or about a thumb knuckle over.
- Add next 12 ingredients.
- Stir and cover. Maintain a slow simmer for about 2½ - 3 hours. Stir the pot gently and check beans every hour.
- Taste the beans to see if there is a need to add more seasoning. I also mash a few of the beans on the side of the pot after the second hour and stir a bit. This is a little trick to make the beans creamy.
- Remove from heat and serve over rice.

HINT: Soak your beans on the countertop overnight. Fill up the pot about 4 inches, or enough to completely cover the beans. Never soak the beans on a gas stove! That little bit of heat from the pilot light will heat the beans just enough to potentially sour them. Avoid this, so you don't have to toss the beans!

I do not salt the beans until they've cooked at least 1 hour. If you use a particularly salty meat you can almost avoid the salt altogether.

INGREDIENTS

1-2 pork tenderloins
1½ tsp. Joe's Stuff seasoning
2 tsp. crushed dried rosemary
1 tsp. dried sage
½ cup sweet orange marmalade
3 tbl. Grand Marnier
3 tbl. orange juice

Roast Pork Tenderloin with Orange Glaze

We love pork. As a matter of fact, most Louisianans enjoy pork. It really is a part of our cooking culture. You should know that at 101 years old, my mother, Harriet, is one of those Louisiana ladies that will attest to this.

The pork in this recipe cooks tender in 30 minutes. I include a sweet Louisiana marmalade as a glaze. I've found the orange flavors are the perfect culinary compliment to pork. And, a little Grand Marnier adds spunk and intensity. It's quick and easy. – *Harriet*

Instructions

- Preheat oven to 350°.
- Cut all tough membrane from tenderloins.
- Pat dry and season well on all sides.
- Place meat on a sprayed shallow baking pan. Roast uncovered in oven for ½ to ¾ of an hour.
- Meanwhile, blend together the marmalade, Grand Marnier and orange juice. Heat glaze in the microwave until warmed.
- About 10 minutes before the tenderloins are ready baste the pork.
- When internal meat temperature reaches 150° remove from oven.

HINT: If I have any glaze remaining, I put it all on the tenderloins and then cover loosely with foil and let rest for 15 minutes.

INGREDIENTS

1 box jumbo pasta shells, about 30-35, cook and drain
3 lb. ground meat dressing*
3 cups red gravy* or jar (24 oz.) of Prego (buy 2 large jars of Prego)
¼ cup vermouth
3 cups mozzarella, grated or shredded
1 cup Parmesan cheese, grated or shredded

Stuffed Jumbo Pasta Shells

This is one of those recipes where you can use the Italian sausage and ground meat dressing to create something so new that no one will realize you pulled the meat from the freezer. You see, I'm always thinking ahead just like all of the working ladies out there. And the best advice I can give is to plan ahead with your cooking and make double. It will actually help double your free time. It's just so true.

The "Prego" trick came about when my Italian/French in-laws unexpectedly announced they were coming for dinner. Oops! I had about 30 minutes to make it happen once I got home. And, I know for sure Ma Maw NEVER had red gravy out of a jar before that day. But, she had it that night and loved it. (Yes, I'm smiling.) I stuffed those shells just like the recipe said and poured the store-bought red gravy with a swish of vermouth over them. I have to admit that I hid the jars in the neighbor's garbage can. And, there you go. Topped those shells with the cheese and it was impressive. Don't ask. Don't tell. I'm just telling you.

Another trick with this recipe is to make sure you leave the grocery store with a box of shells that aren't crumbling to pieces. That's pretty frustrating. My trick? Turn that box over and see if shell pieces rain down. Keep checking boxes until you find the perfect intact one. FYI: There are about 33 shells to a box. I've counted! I don't care if you have to go through every box on the shelf to avoid a bunch of broken pieces. Do it! – Harriet

INSTRUCTIONS

- Preheat oven to 350°.
- Prepare a large baking dish by spraying with a cooking spray. Spread a thin layer of red gravy on the bottom.
- Stuff shells with the meat dressing and arrange in the baking pan.
- Heat red gravy or store bought sauce. Swish out jar with vermouth and add to gravy or sauce. Pour over stuffed shells.
- Bake until the sauce is bubbling, about 30 minutes.
- Remove from oven and top with cheese. Pop back in oven for cheese to melt, about 5 minutes. Serve immediately.

*See Lagniappe for Beef and Italian Sausage dressing and Red Gravy recipes.

5

Seafood Entrées

White Beans & Shrimp

My mother's white bean dish came about after she went back to work in the 1950's. I was in high school and I'm pretty sure she went back to cover my tuition at Mount Carmel. She would do white beans on Saturday to give herself a little break. Daddy's contribution was the shrimp. Of course, the shrimp wasn't from a trip to the grocery store. No sir! His routine was fishing on Saturday. And, heaven forbid if it rained. If Daddy could fish, we knew everything was right and good in the world.

Daddy fished with live shrimp bait! That unused bait didn't go in the water when the fishing day was over. No way! Daddy came back home with his speckled trout bonanza. Momma and I would take the leftover bait, peel the shrimp and she would add it to the white beans. You can't imagine how delicious it was. A sunny day meant we had less shrimp. A rainy day, loads of those little gems filled the bean pot. Either way, we were all happy. - *Harriet*

INGREDIENTS

- 1 lb. white beans, soaked overnight, drained for cooking
- 2 qt. water to cover beans
- 2 tbl. bacon fat
- 4 cups onion, finely chopped
- 2 cups celery, finely chopped
- 1 cup green bell pepper, finely chopped
- 1 tsp. thyme
- 2-3 bay leaves
- 4 toes (cloves) garlic, finely chopped
- 1 lb. smoked ham hock
- 2 tbl. Joe's Stuff seasoning
- 2-3 tbl. chicken or ham base – to taste.
- 1 lb. 50/60 count shrimp, peeled, heads and tails removed and deveined
- ½ cup each parsley and green onions, finely chopped for cooking and garnish

INSTRUCTIONS

- In a large stockpot, add soaked beans and cover with water. The water level should be one inch over beans or about a thumbnail over.
- Add the next 12 ingredients, stir well.
- Maintain a slow simmer for about 2 ½ - 3 hours. Stir the pot gently and check beans every ½ hour. Taste the beans to see if there is a need to add more seasoning. I also mash a few of the beans on the side of the pot after the second hour and stir a bit into the pot. This is a little trick to make the beans creamy.
- About 10 minutes before the beans are ready to serve, stir in the shrimp, cover and simmer. Remove from heat and serve over rice and top with chopped parsley and green onions.

INGREDIENTS

¾ stick butter
½ lb. fresh button mushrooms, rough chopped
½ cup onions, finely chopped
½ cup red bell pepper, finely chopped
3 toes (cloves) garlic, finely chopped
4 tbl. all-purpose flour
1½ cups heavy cream
½ cup Parmesan cheese, finely grated and divided in half
2 tbl. Joe's Stuff seasoning or more to taste
¼-¾ tsp. cayenne, more or less to taste
½ bunch green onions, finely chopped
1 lb. lump crabmeat
¼ cup cream sherry or to taste
4-6 ramekins depending on the size of your portions

Crabmeat Au Gratin

Dishes made "au gratin" refer to a classic French cooking technique that involves baking or cooking under the broiler and ending up with a crusty topping of cheese. Here in New Orleans, the most famous of the gratin dishes is definitely with crab meat. Talk about rich and delicious. You'll want to lick the pot. No kidding! I love the way this dish evolved to feature crab meat. It just makes it so New Orleans. I always serve this with crusty French bread and a light salad. C'est bon! — *Anne*

INSTRUCTIONS

- Preheat broiler or oven to 450°.
- In a large skillet on a medium fire, melt the butter and add the mushrooms. Sauté until they begin to brown about 8-10 minutes. Remove from skillet.
- Add the onions and the red bell pepper. Continue to sauté until the onions are transparent, about 5 minutes. Add the garlic, sauté 2 minutes. Return mushrooms to skillet.
- Lower the fire to medium and slowly whisk in the flour to make a blonde roux. Cook for 4-5 minutes stirring the entire time.
- Push all the ingredients to the side of the skillet. Slowly pour the cream and ¼ cup of Parmesan cheese into the center of the skillet.
- Allow it to warm up then blend into the roux.
- Gradually add in the remaining ingredients except for the crab meat, sherry and remaining Parmesan cheese. Blend well.
- Add the crabmeat and stir in gently so as to not break up the lump crab meat.
- Add sherry and adjust seasonings if needed. Remove from heat.
- Ladle into individual ramekins (4-6) and top off with the remaining cheese.
- Place ramekins under broiler or in oven until the tops begin to brown slightly.

INGREDIENTS

6 puff pastry shells (Pepperidge Farm makes them)

4 tbl. butter

1 bunch green onions, finely chopped

1 bunch parsley, finely chopped

4 toes (cloves) garlic, finely chopped

2 cups heavy cream

¾ cup smoked Gouda cheese, shredded

2 tsp. Joe's Stuff seasoning or more to taste

¼ tsp. cayenne - start off with a quarter teaspoon- you want a subtle kick

1 lb. Louisiana crawfish tails*. (Whatever you do, don't get Chinese crawfish tails. Spanish is okay. Read the label carefully. These companies are sneaky. They'll repackage and put a Cajun name on it.)

½ cup cream sherry

Crawfish & Cheese in Puff Pastry

One of my dearest friends in New Orleans is a priest, affectionately known as Pere Roux. Can you believe the luck of that last name in New Orleans? So as not to disappoint, I want to share that Father Roux is an amazing gourmet cook. God gave him his name rightly! On the occasion of his first dinner with us, I served puff pastry filled with crawfish and cheese. I was so happy when he raved over my dish. The best part of the story is when Pere Roux told me during Sunday Mass the next day as the choir was singing, all he could think about was how good the meal was. I asked him if he had to go to confession for that! *– Anne*

INSTRUCTIONS

- Preheat oven to 350°.
- Bake pastry shells according to directions. Discard center portion after baked. Keep warm.
- In a large skillet, melt the butter over a medium fire. Add the green onions, parsley and garlic. Sauté three minutes.
- Slowly blend in the cream, cheese and seasonings. Stir continuously until the cheese melts. Add the remaining ingredients except the crawfish. Continue cooking until the sauce thickens enough to coat the back of the spoon.
- Add the crawfish and sherry. Cook for 5 minutes. Adjust seasonings if necessary
- Ladle hot crawfish mixture directly into the pastry shells and serve. It's okay if some dribbles out and over – it's picturesque!

*This would also work well with shrimp and both work well over pasta.

INGREDIENTS

2 cups stock (crawfish, seafood, clam or chicken)
2½ sticks butter, divided
1 cup onions, finely chopped
1 cup red or green bell peppers, finely chopped
1 heaping tsp. tomato paste
6-8 toes (cloves) garlic, finely chopped
½ cup all-purpose flour
2 lb. crawfish tail meat (use Louisiana crawfish if possible; Spanish is okay, but never Chinese!)
2 tbl. Joe's Stuff seasoning
Pinch cayenne (you can always add more)
½ bunch parsley, finely chopped
½ stick butter cut into pats for the creaming of the gravy
½ bunch green onions, finely chopped
Rice for serving

Crawfish Étouffée

I thought long and hard before including this recipe in our book because it has many memories, not all good. But I discussed it with my son Tommy and he gave me the go-ahead.

Here's how the story goes. Shelby Ryan Leonhard was our oldest grandchild. She was a sweetheart of a girl with a vibrant "joie de vivre" look at life. When she was in the 7th grade she volunteered to make Crawfish Etouffee for the class since they were studying crustaceans. She enlisted my help but I insisted she do all the work.

Shelby and I cooked it with homemade crawfish stock, the way it's done at K-Paul's Restaurant. It was OUTSTANDING! I always say if I can choose where my last meal will be, it would be there. The entire family raved about it. She was so proud of her accomplishment. I remember her saying to me at the table, "Grandma, if you can't make it to K-Paul's for your last meal, I'll fix it for you!" We all laughed.

Well life doesn't always turn out the way you hope. Shelby died of cancer two years later. I will always remember this with a smile and tears. (I'm tearing as I'm writing this.) –Anne

INSTRUCTIONS

- In a saucepan, heat stock on medium heat. Keep warm.
- In a Dutch oven, melt one stick of butter on a medium heat.
- Sauté the onions and bell pepper until onions are transparent, about 5-8 minutes.
- Add the tomato paste and garlic. Cook for 5 minutes then reduce heat to keep warm.
- In a large skillet melt another stick of butter for the roux. Add the flour and whisk continuously on medium fire until a medium brown color. Immediately add the roux to the vegetable mixture.
- Slowly add the warm stock and blend. Boil gently until the gravy begins to thicken. Add the crawfish tail meat, Joe's Stuff seasoning, cayenne and parsley. Heat for 5 minutes and adjust seasoning if necessary.
- Turn off the heat and begin to cream the gravy by adding the remaining half stick of butter, 1 pat of butter at a time to the gravy whisking so the butter will melt. When a pat is almost melted, add another. This gives a beautiful glossy appearance to the gravy.

HINT: Serve over rice and sprinkle with a few green onions for garnish.

ingredients

4 fillets
½ stick butter
4 tbl. vegetable oil or peanut
   oil
   Joe's Stuff seasoning,
   generously sprinkled over
   fillets, top and bottom
1 cup all-purpose flour
¼ cup parsley, finely chopped
   for garnish
1 lemon sliced for garnish

Pan-Frying Fish

New Orleanian cooks have elevated pan-frying fish to an art. Pan-frying is perfect for light, delicate fish like speckled trout. Speckled trout is found in the waterways surrounding New Orleans. I grew up eating it. And still today fishermen from all walks of life love to trade stories about where to fish the coming weekend to find the "specs running." Even though you find it in abundance, fresh speckled trout is beloved. Top it off with a Meuniére or Almondine sauce* and voila!

We aren't necessarily into fishing at the Leonhard house. But, all of us love to eat fish. And, I enjoy cooking fish. My fortunate luck is having a friend, Darilyn who along with her husband and son are avid fishermen. But, here is the best part, they really don't eat much fish. Priceless! Just like a bartender that doesn't drink. Needless to say we have a great relationship! It's not unheard of on a Sunday for Darilyn to call and offer us the fresh catch. I always race right over. She and her family are over the top gracious with ice chests loaded with baggies of cleaned and filleted fish. I lovingly refer to her as my fish monger. This is my tribute and continued thanks for keeping me stocked. It's simply the best.

Pan-frying is my favorite way to prepare and eat trout. You'll want a good skillet. I use a cast iron skillet about 12" wide and 2" deep. Make sure you warm the platter receiving the fish - this way the fish won't stick to it after you've cooked them.

In addition to having a good skillet it is really helpful to have a fish spatula. A fish spatula is a longer shape slotted spatula usually with a razor thin edge design specifically to turn delicate fish while cooking. You can pick up one at any home or cookware store. – Anne

INSTRUCTIONS

- Warm the platter in a low oven until ready to use.
- Rinse the fillets under cool water and pat dry with paper towels. Set aside.
- Melt butter in oil over medium high heat. It's ready when a speck of flour dropped in oil begins to sizzle.
- Season fillets on both sides, dredge in flour and shake off excess.
- Fry immediately – approximately 2 minutes per side until a golden brown. Remove, drain on paper towel and place on warmed platter.

*See Lagniappe section for sauce recipes.

ingredients

2 sticks butter for sautéing,
   divided in half
1 medium onion, finely
   chopped
½ bunch green onions,
   finely chopped
5 toes (cloves) garlic, finely
   chopped
½ cup all-purpose flour
2 lb. raw, completely peeled
   shrimp
1 (6 oz.) can tomato paste
2 bell peppers, finely
   chopped
1 tbl. Joe's Stuff seasoning
   or more to taste
2 cups warmed shrimp
   stock or warmed chicken
   stock regular strength

Shrimp Creole

Our friend, Ann, comes from a small town in southern Illinois. We tease her about being a Yankee, but in truth she only lived there for 21 years. So, she's definitely a New Orleanian. Ann doesn't particularly like to cook and God knows she didn't grow up eating Gulf of Mexico shrimp; but the strange thing is that she excels at making this dish. This recipe was given to her over 50 years ago by an old matron in her garden club.

It's absolutely the best Shrimp Creole I have ever had in my life - better than Mama's! This recipe does do things differently from the usual way, but it's so good I am afraid to change it. What's so surprising about this recipe is that it's made with twice as many bell peppers as onions. I normally do not like green bell peppers but in this recipe it is essential.

Also amazing is that the shrimp are cooked so long. It doesn't make them mushy, so follow these directions. I do think you need shrimp stock for the ultimate flavor. – *Anne*

INSTRUCTIONS

- In a Dutch oven, melt 1 stick of butter over medium-high heat.
- Add the regular onions and sauté until translucent, about 5 minutes.
- Add the green onions and garlic. Continue to sauté for another two minutes.
- Lower fire to medium and add flour to make the roux, stirring continuously. Cook to a caramel color, about 8-10 minutes.
- Add the remaining stick of butter and stir to melt. Add the shrimp and stir to thoroughly coat the shrimp with the roux. (Note: the mixture will look a little funky…keep going and don't worry!)
- Add the tomato paste, green peppers, Joe's Stuff seasoning. Continue to cook for 15 minutes. Keep stirring to keep the mixture from sticking to the pot.
- After 15 minutes, pour in the warmed stock and blend. At this point it is a relief because the liquid makes it easier to stir. Continue cooking another 10 minutes, stirring often.
- Reduce heat to simmer and cook about 35 minutes more. Yes - I told you this recipe is different.
- Serve over rice.

ingredients

- 2 sticks butter, one for sautéing, the other for pan frying
- 1 medium onion, finely chopped
- 1 large red bell pepper, finely chopped
- 4 toes (cloves) garlic, finely chopped
- ½ bunch green onions, finely chopped
- ½ bunch parsley, finely chopped
- ½ loaf STALE French bread, broken up, moistened and squeezed of excess water (about 2½ cups, loosely packed)
- ½ cup Parmesan cheese, finely grated
- 2 tbl. Joe's Stuff seasoning (or to taste)
- ½ tsp. cayenne pepper (or to taste)
- ½ tsp. salt
- 1 lb. claw meat (it's cheaper and sweeter than lump; canned is acceptable)
- 2 eggs, well beaten
- 3 cups Panko bread crumbs

Crab Cakes

Nowadays crab cakes are on menus all around town. That term didn't exist when we were growing up. The crab mixture was stuffed in a crab shell and called stuffed crab. In the 1980's Emeril came to town and introduced a new term to our vocabulary.

When you prepare these I think it is ESSENTIAL that you serve them with my daughter Beth's Tiger Sauce! *– Anne*

INSTRUCTIONS

- In a large skillet, melt one stick of butter over medium high heat. Sauté onion and bell pepper about five minutes.
- Add garlic, green onions and parsley. Continue sautéing for two minutes.
- Add the French bread, cheese and seasonings. Stir well to blend. Gently fold in the crab meat.
- Remove from heat. Transfer to a large bowl and allow to cool for about 20 minutes.
- Add the eggs and lightly mix (I use my hands). Refrigerate about an hour. The mixture will be easier to handle as the butter firms up. If you are still having a hard time add a little dry Italian flavored bread crumbs.
- Shape crab cakes into small hamburger-size patties, about 3 inches. Press into Panko bread crumbs to coat patties on both sides. Fry immediately on medium-high in the butter. Cook until browned on both sides.

*See Lagniappe for recipe of Tiger Sauce

6
Vegetables

Creamed Spinach

I personally adore this dish. For years, I made it in an attempt to coax my children into what we were told was an iron rich vegetable. I assured the kids that "Someday you are going to love it!" Sure enough, that came to pass. Some of my grandchildren are still in the "I don't like it stage" but I know it's only a matter of time. – *Anne*

INGREDIENTS

2 (10 oz.) pkg. frozen chopped spinach
½ stick butter
1 (8 oz.) pkg. Philadelphia cream cheese, softened
½ tsp. salt, or to taste

TOPPING:

½ stick butter
¾ cup Italian flavored bread crumbs

INSTRUCTIONS

- Cook the spinach according to the directions and drain well.
- In a medium size saucepan, melt ½ stick of butter.
- Add softened cream cheese and stir to fully melt and incorporate.
- Add the drained, cooked spinach and blend well. Add salt to taste.

TOPPING:

- In a small saucepan, melt the butter over low heat. Remove from fire.
- Stir in bread crumbs until all the butter is absorbed.

- Preheat oven to 350°.
- Put spinach mixture in an 8" x 8" open casserole.
- Cover with bread crumb topping.
- Bake about 20-25 minutes or until bread crumbs begin to brown.

Carrot Soufflé

I cherish this recipe. Hands down, it is one of my favorites and I am so happy to share it with you. It was given to me by Abe Stackhouse. Abe and I worked together for 24 years at East Jefferson General Hospital. He was the Head Chef. His imagination for creating recipes from a simple description of a dish I might have enjoyed at a restaurant was uncanny. He was always concocting dishes and twists on recipes that were unmatched. Abe had the ability to pair ingredients for a fantastic outcome. I would never try to tell you that this recipe is a healthy choice. It just has a fantastic flavor, a wonderful treat! – *Harriet*

INGREDIENTS

3 lb. fresh carrots, washed, peeled and sliced
3 sticks butter
6 large eggs
½ cup all-purpose flour
1 tbl. baking powder
3 cups white granulated sugar
3 tbl. vanilla extract
Confectioners sugar for dusting

INSTRUCTIONS

- Preheat oven to 350°.
- Boil carrots until tender in lightly salted water, drain.
- Mash carrots by hand, mixer or food processor until smooth. Add remaining ingredients, except confectioners sugar and process until smooth.
- Pour into a 3 qt. greased baking dish, bake until set and lightly brown about 1 hour.
- Dust with confectioners sugar.

Smothered Cabbage with Apples

It is a tradition in New Orleans to have cabbage any which way on the table for New Year's Day. When you "smother", you are simmering on low heat and the food collapses after a long cooking time on low heat. What it does to the food is add a sweetness. Cabbage really reacts great to this technique. I love to add apples or pears. You can eat this alone or serve it with pork or even steak. Everyone will feel lucky to eat this no matter the time of year.
- Harriet

INGREDIENTS

2-3 fresh apples or pears or a combination of both, rough chopped, peeling optional

2 medium onions, finely chopped

1 lb. ham pieces

2 tbl. bacon fat

1 small-medium cabbage head, roughly chopped

¼ cup vinegar, fruit flavored such as pear

¼ cup light brown sugar

½ tsp. pepper or to taste

INSTRUCTIONS

• Sauté fruit, onions and ham pieces in bacon fat for about 3-4 minutes.
• Add cabbage, vinegar, brown sugar and pepper.
• Stir to combine and cook until cabbage is tender, as you like it.

ingredients

½ stick butter
¼ cup pure maple syrup*
¼ tsp. salt
⅛ tsp. cayenne pepper
1½ lb. peeled carrots, sliced
   on a diagonal

Maple Glazed Carrots

This recipe is perfect. And, you have to include the cayenne pepper. Even with the smallest amount, it makes a difference if you leave it out. This recipe is my grandchildren's favorite vegetable. Hallelujah!

Cute story . . . I thought it would be a good idea to add a little sprinkle of chopped parsley as a decorative garnish. It really did look pretty with the bright orange of the carrots glistening from the glaze and the bright pop of green color. Picture worthy. But as children are apt to do, my grandson Resse, about three years old at the time said, "Grandma, I don't like grass on my carrots!" That was the end of my creativity with this dish and a reminder from the mouth of babes not to mess with perfection. – *Anne*

INSTRUCTIONS

- In a large saucepan, melt butter over medium heat. Add syrup, salt and cayenne.
- Add carrots. Bring to a boil, partially cover and reduce to a simmer. Simmer for 15-20 minutes or until carrots are fork tender. Stir occasionally to make sure carrots are coated. The liquid will thicken.
- Remove from heat and serve.

*Use real maple syrup. The imitation syrup is not rich enough. Also, include the cayenne pepper. It mellows out the sweetness of the syrup in the most subtle way. I left it out once and it really did not taste as good. Slicing the carrots on a diagonal makes for a beautiful presentation. If the carrots are cooked and the sauce has not thickened enough, remove carrots to serving dish and continue to cook until sauce is thick. Pour over carrots for service.

Stuart

ingredients

1 tbl. bacon fat

2 tbl. butter

½ lb. good flavored sausage, diced

1 medium onion, finely chopped

1 medium red bell pepper, seeded and white parts removed, finely chopped

3 tsp. Joe's Stuff seasoning

3 toes (cloves) garlic, smashed and finely chopped

2-3 cups corn (frozen or fresh off the cob)

2 medium tomatoes, peeled and seeded

½ lb. okra, cut into wheels and tops removed

½ cup chicken or vegetable broth (optional)

Maque Choux

My maternal grandmother, Georgeanne Deacon, had a garden at her home on the corner of Constance and Octavia just off Jefferson and Magazine. She was an Uptown girl who grew okra, garlic, bell peppers, parsley, tomatoes and green onion. Essentially, it was a true Creole garden. The only thing she didn't grow was the corn. We bought the corn from our neighborhood truck vendor as he passed by the house. I remember the truck passing almost everyday. This was before supermarkets existed. What a great memory!

The corn my mother used for maque choux was fresh and sweet and is the backbone of the recipe. It is said that maque choux is a recipe from the Native Americans. I like to call them the first families of America, the original settlers of New Orleans. This is a true taste of New Orleans history.
— *Harriet*

INSTRUCTIONS

- Sauté first seven ingredients until onions are tender and translucent, about 5 minutes.
- Add corn, tomatoes and okra. Simmer until okra is tender, about 20 minutes.
- If liquid cooks down, add chicken or vegetable broth to keep the ingredients from sticking to the pan.
- Adjust seasonings to taste.

ingredients

¼ cup apple juice or a citrus
  juice combination
3 tsp. rice vinegar
3 tbl. olive oil
1 tsp. salt
4 tbl. melted butter
1 tsp. sage
1 tsp. crushed rosemary
1 tsp. thyme
1 acorn squash, peeled,
  seeded and cut into
  wedges or cubed
1 butternut squash, peeled,
  seeded and cut into
  wedges or cubed
1 small cooking pumpkin,
  peeled, seeded and cut
  into wedge or cubed

Roasted Vegetables

Thanksgiving 2005 was difficult for many families in the New Orleans area. Everyone in my family (except my son Peter and I) lost everything in Hurricane Katrina. This city is a survivor. New Orleanians have met many disasters and risen to the top. We celebrate each and every holiday, even Mardi Gras. We realized life had to go on and celebrating is a big part of what we do. The first Thanksgiving after Hurricane Katrina, my entire family came to my home. The day was beautiful. We all ate outside and of course gave a special thanks to life, family and New Orleans. — *Harriet*

INSTRUCTIONS

- Preheat oven to 400°.
- Combine everything in a large zip lock plastic bag, seal and shake to coat vegetables.
- Place vegetables on a jelly roll pan lined with parchment or spray with non-stick spray.
- Place in the oven and bake for 25 minutes or more until vegetables are golden and tender. Turn halfway through cooking to ensure each piece cooks through.

HINT: Any combination of vegetables will be delicious, try the winter squash variety for a change.

ingredients

1 stick butter
2 large eggplants peeled
and rough chopped
1 cup water
½ stick butter for sautéing
1 cup onions, finely
chopped
4 toes (cloves) garlic
pressed or finely chopped
¾ lb. medium sized shrimp,
boiled, completely peeled
and rough chopped
1 cup (or more if needed)
moistened stale French
bread crumbs (squeeze
excess water out with
your hands)
½ bunch parsley, finely
chopped
2 tbl. Joe's Stuff seasoning
(or more to taste)
¼ tsp. salt
¼ tsp. cayenne
½ cup Parmesan cheese,
finely grated
¼ cup Parmesan cheese
finely grated for topping
off casserole
A few pats of butter for
topping

Stuffed Eggplant

Eggplant is easy to grow in South Louisiana and very abundant. Although not native to North America the eggplant plays a big role in our cultural cuisine here. The French gave us Ratatouille and the Italians gave us Eggplant Parmesan.

Harriet and I both grew up with stuffed eggplant. Her mother, Ms. Harriet, actually stuffed the eggplant shell while my mother peeled it and put the "meat" in a casserole. – *Anne*

INSTRUCTIONS

- Preheat oven to 350°.
- In a large saucepan, melt butter over medium heat. Add peeled eggplant and water. Cover, reduce heat to low and cook until eggplant is very tender and almost mushy, about 10-15 minutes.
- Remove from heat, drain and mash eggplant. Set aside
- In a large skillet melt ½ stick of butter over medium heat. Sauté onions until transparent, about five minutes. Add garlic and cook two more minutes.
- Add mushy eggplant to the onion and garlic mix. Add shrimp, French bread, parsley, seasonings and ½ cup of Parmesan cheese. Taste and adjust seasonings.
- Remove from skillet and transfer to a buttered 8" x 8" casserole. Top with remaining ¼ cup Parmesan cheese and a few pats of butter.
- Bake in oven until heated through, about 20 minutes.

HINT: You could always add 1 lb. of claw crabmeat (canned is fine), in addition to the shrimp.

ingredients

5 large ripe Creole
  tomatoes or bell peppers
1 stick butter
1½ cups onion, finely
  chopped
2 tbl. garlic, finely chopped
1 tsp. Italian seasoning
3 tbl. Joe's Stuff seasoning
  (or more to taste) divided
  into two portions
¼ tsp. cayenne
  contents of hollowed out
  tomatoes, if using, rough
  chopped
1 bunch parsley, finely
  chopped
1½ lbs. raw shrimp
  completely peeled, rough
  chopped
2 cups stale French bread,
  moistened and squeezed
  out
½ cup Parmesan cheese,
  finely grated
¼ cup Parmesan cheese for
  topping off
5 pats butter

Stuffed Tomatoes & Peppers

When we were growing up, Creole tomatoes and bell peppers became available in the late spring. Mama would stuff them with shrimp and sometimes crab meat. This was a traditional item on Sunday dinner tables for many New Orleanians. – *Anne*

INSTRUCTIONS

- Preheat oven to 350°.
- Cut bell peppers in half horizontally. Remove stems and seeds. Par-boil until slightly tender. If using tomatoes, cut off stems, scoop out the pulp and rough chop.
- Melt butter in a large skillet on a medium heat. Sauté the onions until transparent. Add garlic, ½ of the Joe's Stuff and sauté remainder of seasonings. Sauté 5 minutes.
- If using tomatoes, add the pulp and cook until softened.
- Meanwhile, season shrimp with remaining Joe's Stuff. Add to vegetable mix in skillet. When the shrimp turn pink they're cooked. If using crab meat, now is the time to add it. (1 lb. is perfect.)
- Add the French bread and ½ cup of the Parmesan cheese. Blend well. Adjust seasoning if needed.
- Stuff the tomatoes and bell peppers. Sprinkle on the remaining cheese and top with a pat of butter.
- Bake for 20 minutes.

7
Sides

Baked Rice

Our generation grew up eating rice in South Louisiana as our primary starch. We would have potatoes a few times a month. But today it's all different. Potatoes are as common as rice on our dinner plates.

Rice is grown extensively in South Louisiana. Interesting fact – crawfish are raised in the same fields as rice just at a different time of the year. Two different "crops" from the same fields. How convenient!

Mama used long grain rice. The kernels are very starchy on the outside. I can still see her with the colander in the sink running water over the rice until the water ran clear. Nan, on the other hand, would use Uncle Ben's. It doesn't have to be washed. That's primarily what I use. Basmati would work well also, but you'll need to wash it.

This is a really easy recipe. It makes for a pretty presentation. I think you'll enjoy it. – *Anne*

INGREDIENTS

- ½ stick butter
- ½ lb. fresh mushrooms, thinly sliced (Nan used canned because in those days fresh mushrooms weren't available.)
- 1 cup rice, uncooked
- 1 (10 oz.) can onion soup, undiluted
- 1 (10 oz.) can beef bouillion, undiluted
- 1 (5 oz.) can drained, sliced water chestnuts

INSTRUCTIONS

- Preheat oven to 350°.
- Melt butter in skillet.
- Sauté mushrooms in butter until browned. Combine all ingredients in casserole.
- Cover and bake for 45 minutes. If you find the rice too wet, uncover and continue baking a few minutes longer until excess liquid evaporates.

Baked Beans

What's a barbecue without baked beans? Nan had a recipe that beat them all! I've shared it with so many people, I can't count!   Whenever we barbecue we have this along with Nan's Green Bean Salad. – Anne

INGREDIENTS

- 1 (55 oz.) can Bush's Baked Beans with juice
- ¼ cup mustard seeds
- 1 (6 oz.) can french fried onion rings
- 1 lb. raw bacon cut into small pieces
- 1 cup light brown sugar

INSTRUCTIONS

- Preheat oven to 300°.
- In a large casserole, simply create layers of the above ingredients in the order that are listed. You should have at least three distinctive layers.
- Cover and bake for 4 hours.

Garlic Scalloped Potatoes

This is a decadently delicious dish that Robert and Carolyn, (my husband's brother and his wife) would make for our Saturday night suppers. It is really rich - that is an understatement! If there are any leftovers, they can be pureed with a little milk and made into a potato soup.

When you read this you're probably going to gasp at the amount of rich ingredients – but just remember we don't eat this everyday. So, for a special occasion why not splurge! Just don't tell anyone about the rich ingredients. – *Anne*

INGREDIENTS

5 medium brown potatoes

6-8 toes (cloves) garlic, finely chopped

Joe's Stuff seasoning to sprinkle

1 stick butter

1 qt. heavy cream (However, you probably won't use it all.)

INSTRUCTIONS

- Preheat oven to 350°.
- In a large casserole, simply create layers of the above ingredients in the order that are listed. You should have at least three distinctive layers.
- Pour the cream over the potatoes until you've reached halfway up the sides of the casserole
- Bake uncovered for ¾ - 1 hour, until the potatoes are fork tender.

Hot Curry Fruit Casserole

I've been making this recipe since the early 70's. I had it at a Revellion party and it was such a surprise of flavors. Traditionally, Revellion was the celebratory dinner enjoyed after Midnight Mass on Christmas Eve. In New Orleans, we like to stretch things out. Now, our Revellion dinners begin a few weeks before Christmas Day at our restaurants and end after Midnight Mass for many families around the city.

From the first bite, my culinary imagination ran wild. I realized if I made it for dinner, the next day I had a topping for pancakes or waffles. You could just even eat it by itself and add a dollop of sour cream. – Harriet

INGREDIENTS

- 1 (12 oz.) can peaches, drained
- 1 (12 oz.) can pears, drained
- 1 (12 oz.) can apricots, drained
- 1 (12 oz.) can pineapple chunks, drained
- 1 (12 oz.) can Bing cherries, drained
- ½ cup dried blueberries
- ½ cup dried cranberries
- 1½ sticks butter
- 1 cup light brown sugar
- 2 tsp. curry powder
- ½ tsp. ground ginger

INSTRUCTIONS

- Preheat oven to 350°.
- Place fruit in a 3 qt. buttered casserole dish.
- In a saucepan over medium heat, melt butter, add sugar, curry powder and ground ginger. Blend thoroughly.
- Pour over fruit.
- Bake for 45 minutes until juices are bubbly.

Sweet Potatoes with Praline Topping

My daughter-in-law, Jan (Tommy's wife), is not exactly known for her culinary prowess. She does however, love to make desserts and is quite good at that. She really puts out some pretty presentations. But there is one dish that Jan does for the holiday tables—baked sweet potato with this divine pecan laden topping. It's the best I have ever tasted. Harriet and I served it one time on the Steve Harvey Show. It was a big hit! – *Anne*

INGREDIENTS

5 medium sweet
   potatoes (sometimes
   called yams)
¾ cup sugar
1 tbl. good vanilla
½ cup whole milk
2 large eggs, beaten
½ cup butter, melted

PRALINE TOPPING:

1 cup light brown sugar
⅓ cup softened butter
⅓ cup all-purpose flour
1 cup chopped pecans

INSTRUCTIONS

• Preheat the oven to 350°.
• Bake whole potatoes until soft. Peel and mash well.
• Mix all ingredients together in a bowl then place in a greased 9"x13" open casserole.
• Top with Praline Topping and bake uncovered for 30 minutes.

PRALINE TOPPING:

• Mix everything together and spread over the sweet potato mixture.

8

Beverages

Bourbon Slush

During the Holiday Season from the middle of November though Mardi Gras, my younger sisters always faithfully stock their freezers with Tupperware containers of Bourbon Slush. This recipe is simply fantastic and captures in a very grown up way an adult version of our beloved New Orleans snowball. It's a very fun way to have a refreshing cocktail. And, this version has livened up a bridal shower or two in the springtime.

The alcohol keeps this from freezing solid. Plan on making it several days ahead of time to achieve the slush like texture. You can substitute rum for the Bourbon and even add different fruit if you choose. – *Anne*

INGREDIENTS

- 1 liter Bourbon... No need to use the good stuff (you could also substitute rum).
- 1 (2 liter) 7-Up
- 1 (48 oz.) can pineapple juice
- 1 (8 oz.) can crushed pineapple including juice
- 1 (6 oz.) can condensed frozen orange juice, undiluted
- 1 (16 oz.) jar Maraschino cherries and juice, chopped

INSTRUCTIONS

- In a large pot, mix all ingredients together.
- Divide mixture evenly into 2-gallon sized containers. Place in freezer.
- Stir about 4 times a day for 2 - 3 days to keep the fruit in suspension.

Then it's ready to serve.

ingredients

1 large pineapple peeled
  and cut into bite-sized
  pieces
2 (16 oz.) containers
  strawberries (fresh or
  frozen)
1 fifth brandy
1 fifth good bourbon,
  chilled
2 bottles champagne
  (750ml each) to get
  started, chilled

Forbidden Fruit Punch

Forbidden . . . Well that's part of the story for sure. But let me start by saying that a friend, Karen, makes this punch perfectly. And, she usually makes it around the holidays.

Our ritual for years was a big family gathering during the holidays. Everyone showed up to eat and drink. And, I mean everyone! And, like all good Catholics, we aren't against a drink or two. One of my aunts is a Catholic nun. And, certainly in her grace and good judgment, my aunt knows her limits. One holiday after having a couple of drinks she decided she should stop for the day. But, the punch was so good she couldn't resist the delicious fruits Karen had floating in the punch. Well, little did she know the fruit had been macerated in brandy. Needless to say our aunt, who shall remain nameless, never knew what hit her! - *Anne*

INSTRUCTIONS

- Put pineapple and strawberries in a large Tupperware container.
- Cover with brandy, seal container with lid and place in the refrigerator.
- Keep refrigerated for two days.

TO SERVE:

In a large punch bowl, combine chilled bourbon and chilled champagne. Add fruit and brandy. Stir to mix. Serve over ice and garnish with fruit.

As liquid dwindles keep adding champagne. Be cautious of the fruit, it is full of liquor and can be a big surprise! The gift that keeps on giving!

ingredients

1 fifth rum (dark or clear)
1½ cups passion fruit syrup
1½ cups freshly squeezed
   lemon juice
1 cup ice cubes
1 orange sliced for garnish
1 (9 oz.) jar Maraschino
   cherries and juice for
   garnish

Old Fashioned Hurricane

The only storm we ever rode out in New Orleans was Hurricane Issac in 2012. I didn't pack a bag. I didn't bring any food. I just packed Mamma and the fixin's for a good old Hurricane and headed over to my daughter, Victoria's house. She had electricity which meant television and air-conditioning. Television, so you can track the storm, is a priority. And, a/c because do I need to tell you that it's hot as Hades during August in New Orleans. And, that's the truth. - Harriet

INSTRUCTIONS

- Mix all ingredients in a pitcher, let sit for 15 minutes.
- Serve over ice and garnish with a slice of orange and a cherry.

Enjoy!

INGREDIENTS

- 1 (48 oz.) can Hawaiian Punch, original
- 1 (48 oz.) can pineapple juice
- 1 qt. refrigerated orange juice

Punch for Kids

This recipe came from the 60's and 70's when my children started school. What comes with the start of school? Brownies and Cub Scouts. Believe me, we participated in everything! I led the Brownies, Girl Scouts and Cub Scouts! I brought a gallon size pickle jar home from work and it became my "go to" mixing urn for this recipe. It seemed that the punch always tasted better the next day although it never lasted very long! A great idea is to take the leftovers and freeze in ice cube trays as a quick, refreshing snack for the kids. If you need to serve a larger group, take some of the punch and freeze in a bundt pan and add to the punch bowl. It keeps it cool without diluting the punch! I know, pretty old fashioned. But some things are just timeless and good. - Harriet

INSTRUCTIONS

• Mix all together in a gallon container.

INGREDIENTS

PINA COLADA SLUSH:

1 (46 oz.) can pineapple juice

2 (12 oz.) cans frozen lemonade concentrate, thawed and undiluted

3 cups water

2 cups light colored rum

1 (15 oz.) can cream of coconut

2 (2 Liter) lemon lime carbonated beverage, chilled

St. Peter Street Adult Snoballs

Parties in the summertime mean "stoop" parties in the French Quarter. You sit right outside on your doorstep watching the pedestrians and striking up conversations. Many times our stoop parties turned into big pot luck dinners.

Part of summertime here in New Orleans includes the ritual of eating a snowball. Not a snow cone, a snowball! Homemade syrups are poured over shaved ice. The true New Orleans snowball is the texture of real, icy snow, almost like Mother Nature made it herself.

I learned the trick of mixing the flavors and the liquor just the right way to achieve something similar to the legendary frozen New Orleans treat from a tenant in my St. Peter Street apartment. After he moved, I kept the ritual going and kept his furniture too because he stiffed me out of two months rent. I never got to thank him for the recipes! – *Harriet*

Instructions

I use a 2.2 gallon rectangular Rubbermaid container with a lid. The alcohol keeps the mix from freezing all the way. But stir occasionally, until the mixture turns to slush.

Pina Colada Slush:
- Combine pineapple juice, frozen lemonade, water, rum, and cream of coconut.
- Freeze at least 8 hours. Stir several times during the freezing process to keep slush blended.
- When ready to serve remove from freezer.
- Break up and add the lemon lime beverage.
- Stir till slushy and serve.

9
Desserts

Floating Island

Once in a while, Mama would make this beautiful dessert. I can still remember how she served it in a beautiful blue casserole dish. If you've never seen or heard of Floating Island before, you've got to try it. It's basically a liquid custard with puffs ("islands") floating around. – *Anne*

INGREDIENTS

2 cups heavy cream
2 cups half and half
5 large eggs, separated
1 cup granulated sugar
1½ tbl. cornstarch
1 tsp. vanilla
Dash salt
⅛ tsp. cream of tartar
½ cup granulated sugar

FOR THE MERINGUE:
The egg whites
⅛ cream of tartar
½ cup granulated sugar

INSTRUCTIONS

FOR THE CUSTARD:
- Combine cream and half and half. Bring to a simmer.
- Beat the egg yolks in a mixer on high speed until light in color.
- In a separate bowl, mix the sugar and cornstarch together. Add to the egg yolk mixture and blend.
- Very slowly, whisk in the warm cream mixture, a little at a time.
- Pour mixture back into the saucepan cook on medium heat until mixture thickens.
- Add the vanilla and a dash of salt, keep custard warm.

FOR THE ISLANDS (MERINGUE):
- In a mixer on high speed beat the egg whites and cream of tartar until soft peaks form.
- Gradually add the sugar. Continue beating until glossy and really stiff peaks have formed.
- Now you're going to cook the meringue. Drop blobs of meringue into the warmed cream mixture. Cook for 5 minutes on one side and flip over for 2 minutes more. Remove and set aside until ready to serve.

This can be served warm or cold. Mama always served it cold. Regardless, serve in individual bowls with an island of meringue floating on top of the custard.

Blondies

Both of my parents had careers outside the home. My mother perfected the weeknight meal in 30 minutes. Momma was way ahead of Rachel Ray and all the rest of the modern cooking stars. She taught me everything I know about cooking good and cooking fast. While Momma made the main part of the meal, I would work on dessert. This delicious dessert was one of our favorites. And, to this day, I make it fondly remembering what a remarkable woman my mother was.

Today, working families are more the norm than back when I was growing up. I suggest getting the family involved by including everyone in the kitchen creating dinner. It really makes for wonderful memories, teaches kitchen skills and makes families stronger by bonding over food. I think, that to this day, that's why all of my children, Michael, Suzanne, Katherine, Victoria and Peter are all close and stay connected. It started in the kitchen.
– Harriet

INGREDIENTS

- 1 box yellow cake mix
- 3 large eggs beaten (divide: 1 for crust, 2 for filling)
- 1 stick butter, melted
- 1 cup pecan pieces
- 1 (8 oz.) pkg. cream cheese, room temperature
- 1 lb. confectioners sugar

INSTRUCTIONS

- Preheat oven to 350°.
- Combine cake mix, 1 beaten egg, butter and pecans. Press down in the bottom of a greased 9" x 13" pan to form the crust.
- Mix cream cheese, confectioners sugar and remaining two eggs thoroughly. Pour over crust and bake 40 – 45 minutes or until a light golden brown.

Chinese Chew

In my opinion, it takes a real talent to bake desserts. While lots of people cook and add a "little bit more here" or a "little less there", desserts and baking do not work like that. Thank goodness for Aunt Hilda, my mother's oldest sister. Aunt Hilda loved to bake and she was a genius at it. Easter in particular brought out the best in Aunt Hilda's talents. The smell of mincemeat pies wafting from her kitchen is a sweet memory for me.

One of her top treats besides pies was her rendition of a dessert called Chinese Chew. It is simply gooey and good. Where this recipe came from or how it received its unusual name is beyond me. This dessert is a classic and seems to pop up during the holidays as a traditional Christmas treat. I can't relate anything about this recipe that is Chinese whatsoever. But maybe the name came about because it's so exotic and unique. So, who knows and actually who cares . . . but I'm always thinking of things like that! Besides, this recipe is a great showcase for Louisiana pecans. And, we love anything in South Louisiana made with pecans!
- *Anne*

INGREDIENTS

4 large eggs
2 tbl. vanilla
2 cups granulated sugar
1½ cups cake flour
2 tsp. baking powder
¼ tsp. salt
2½ cups chopped pecans
2 cups dates, chopped into small piecesr

INSTRUCTIONS

- Preheat oven to 350°.
- Grease a 9"x 13" inch baking pan with butter.
- In a mixing bowl on medium speed, beat eggs, vanilla and sugar until light and fluffy.
- Sift flour, baking powder and salt over the pecans and dates. (This is important because it keeps the nuts and dates in suspension.)
- Gently fold into the egg and sugar mixture.
- Pour into the greased pan and bake for 40 minutes.
- Remove from oven, cool and cut into squares.

Brownies

On my kitchen wall, I have a framed, faded, handwritten in pencil recipe from my Grandmother and her sister Wizzie for delicious brownies. I love that old time penmanship! I cherish this. When I think of them I can still see them bustling around the kitchen. It always makes me smile. They were quite a team. Grandma was the cook and Wizzie was her assistant.
- Anne

INGREDIENTS

4 large eggs, beaten
2 cups granulated sugar
2 cups all purpose flour, sifted and divided in half
2 tbl. baking powder
2 cups pecans, whole or rough chopped (I prefer rough chopped.)
2 sticks melted butter
4 tbl. cocoa powder
2 tbl. vanilla

ICING:
½ box confectioners sugar
½ stick softened butter
2 tbl. cocoa powder (more if you like it darker)
1 tsp. vanilla
pinch of salt
¼ cup whole milk, just enough milk to get the proper consistency for icing

INSTRUCTIONS

• Preheat oven to 350°.
• Grease an 8"x 8" or 9"x 9" baking pan.
• In a large mixing bowl, combine eggs and sugar.
• Sift in 1 cup of flour with baking powder into egg mixture.
• In a separate bowl filled with the pecans, sift the remaining flour over pecans and toss. This is important because it keeps the pecans in suspension. Set aside.
• In a small saucepan, melt butter over low heat. Add cocoa and combine.
• Gradually add to egg, sugar and flour mixture.
• Add the vanilla and stir. Add coated pecans and thoroughly mix until blended.
• Pour into the greased pan.
• Bake 40 minutes or until a toothpick inserted in the center of the brownies comes out clean. Remove from oven and cool.
• When completely cool, top with icing.

Cocoons

We all have those treats that show up from the neighbors during the holidays. You can mark your calendar for when they arrive on your doorstep, same day and same time every year. These cocoons are one such treat. The texture is soft and crumbly and they aren't too sweet. I was able to commandeer the recipe from my dear neighbor Mrs. Nielsen so I didn't have to wait for them to arrive only once a year. With a sprinkle of confectioner's sugar, enjoy their subtle goodness-but be sure not to wear black when you eat them. - Anne

INGREDIENTS

2 sticks butter, softened
¼ cup confectioners sugar
2 tsp. vanilla
1 tbl. water
2 cups all purpose flour, sifted
1 cup pecans, finely chopped
½-1 cup confectioners sugar for coating

INSTRUCTIONS

- Preheat oven to 350°.
- Using a mixer, cream together butter and sugar on a high speed.
- Lower speed and add vanilla and water. Mix thoroughly.
- Slowly add in flour and then pecans. Mix until blended.
- To make the cookies, take a tablespoon amount of dough, make a small roll about the size of a cocktail hot dog and place on a cookie sheet. Turn the ends slightly toward each other to form a crescent shape.
- Bake for 20 minutes. Remove from oven and while warm, roll in confectioners sugar.

HINT: If you don't want to roll them, then just scoop the batter with a cookie scoop and bake like regular cookies. Still cover with confectioners sugar when finished.

ingredients

1 (8 oz.) pkg. cream cheese, room temperature
1 (14 oz.) can condensed milk (not evaporated)
1 large egg
1 tsp. vanilla
3 tbl. fresh lemon juice
1 cup fresh or frozen raspberries*
1 (6 oz.) prepared chocolate pie crust

Chocolate Raspberry Cream Cheese Pie

This recipe is a Robin family favorite. And, it's a very easy recipe. A testimony to how easy and great it is brings one of my favorite family stories to mind. My daughter-in-law, Geri, not known for her culinary skills, won first place in a dessert contest with this recipe. Puts a smile on my face just to think about it. Yes. It's that good and easy too. – Harriet

Instructions

- Preheat oven to 350°.
- Using a mixer, beat cream cheese until fluffy, on a high speed.
- Gradually beat in condensed milk until smooth.
- Add egg, vanilla and lemon juice, mix well.
- Arrange raspberries over crust and slowly pour cream cheese mixture over berries.
- Bake 30-35 minutes until center is set, cool.

*Save a few berries to decorate the pie after baking.

Irish Cream Cake

I'm 50 percent Irish and I never met an old fashioned cake made with Irish Whiskey I didn't love. Give me a dessert that has Irish Cream in it, move over and cut me a slice. Also, it's not a mistake. Yes. Mayonnaise! It works. Trust me. - *Harriet*

INGREDIENTS

- 1 box devil's food cake mix with pudding
- 4 large eggs
- 1 cup mayonnaise
- 2 cups Irish cream liqueur
- 1 cup chopped pecans
- 1 cup mini marshmallows
- 1 (6 oz.) pkg. chocolate chips of your choice
- Confectioners sugar to sprinkle for garnish

INSTRUCTIONS

- Preheat oven to 350°.
- Grease and flour Bundt or tube pan.
- Set aside 1/2 cup of dry cake mix.
- Mix dry cake mix, eggs, mayonnaise and Irish cream liqueur. Mix well.
- Toss pecans, marshmallow and chocolate chip pieces in the 1/2 cup of dry cake mix. Then fold into the above mixture.
- Pour into prepared pan and bake for 40 - 50 minutes until toothpick inserted in the middle comes out clean.

Cool 10 minutes and invert on a serving plate. When completely cool dust with confectioners sugar.

Wilderness Cookies

Pau Pau A.T., my father-in-law, loved these quasi "nutritious" cookies. He got the recipe from his neighbors who spent a week hiking in Alaska. It really is like a fitness bar without all the preservatives. My son Tommy and his family have a home on the Gulf Coast of Florida. When they go for the week I try to make these cookies for them. It is without a doubt their favorite treat. Even my granddaughter Shelby, who watched her waistline, couldn't control herself when these were around. *- Anne*

INGREDIENTS

- 1 cup Crisco or ½ lb. butter (2 sticks), softened
- 1 cup light brown sugar
- 1 cup granulated sugar
- 2 large eggs
- 1 tsp. vanilla
- 1½ cups all purpose flour, sifted
- 1 tsp. baking soda
- 1 tsp. salt
- 1 cup chopped pecans or almonds
- 3 cups quick Quaker oats
- 1 cup semi-sweet chocolate morsels
- ½ cup grated coconut

INSTRUCTIONS

- Preheat oven to 350°.
- In a large mixing bowl on high speed, cream together Crisco and sugars until light and fluffy.
- Add eggs and vanilla and continue to mix.
- In a separate bowl, sift together flour, baking soda and salt.
- Add the flour to the sugar mixture. Lower speed to medium and continue beating until well blended.
- Add the nuts, oats, chocolate and coconut. Blend well.
- If you don't have a cookie scoop, by all means get one. They make life so much easier in making cookies. I use a 2" scoop.
- Line 2 baking sheets with parchment paper or simply grease them and drop the cookies.
- Bake 10-12 minutes until cookies start to brown. Remove and cool.

In Memory of
Shelby Ryan Leonhard

May 26, 1996 ~ February 15, 2011

ingredients

2 boxes of your favorite brownie mix (include all ingredients listed on the box)

2 cups pecan pieces

1 (10 oz.) bag mini marshmallows

1 (16 oz.) can prepared chocolate cake frosting, melted

Old Man River Mud Cake

This is a recipe I love. Each year, my family gathers at a hotel on St. Charles Avenue for six days leading up to Mardi Gras. I can barely keep track of the number of parades we watch! By the end of Mardi Gras day, it takes a truck to bring us home with our treasured collection of beads and throws from each passing parade. Of course, we cook and bring our food with us to enjoy each day. You would be blown away by the spread - gumbo of all types, jambalayas, fried chicken and this delicious Old Man River Mud Cake for dessert. You know you are welcome to join us if you are in town!
– Harriet

INSTRUCTIONS

- Preheat oven to 350°.
- Prepare brownie mix as directed on box, add pecans. Stir to completely incorporate. Pour batter into a 9"x 13"x2" buttered baking pan and bake according to package directions
- Remove from oven and top with mini marshmallows. Return to oven until marshmallows melt. Remove from oven and top with melted frosting.
- Cool cake completely before cutting.

INGREDIENTS

I use a seasoned deep cast iron skillet.

1 stick butter
1 cup light brown sugar, packed
1 (8 oz.) can pineapple slices, no juice
Maraschino cherries
Pecan halves

SPONGE CAKE:

1 cup cake flour, sifted
¼ tsp. salt
1 tsp. baking powder
4 large eggs, separated
1 cup granulated sugar
2 tbl. melted butter
1 tsp. vanilla extract
1 tsp. almond extract

Pineapple Upside Down Cake

Abby is my youngest granddaughter. She is very much at home in the kitchen like her mother and 2 grandmothers. My son Timothy moved his family to Dallas after Katrina. We're fortunate that they fly us up there several times a year. Abby and I will often cook together. Not too long ago we made my maternal grandmother's pineapple upside cake. – *Anne*

INSTRUCTIONS

- Melt the butter in a cast iron skillet.
- Sprinkle brown sugar around the pan.
- Place pineapple slices on sugar, place cherry in each hole.
- Fill in the open spaces with pecans.

- Preheat oven to 325°.
- Sift together the flour, salt and baking powder. Set aside.
- Separate the egg yolks and whites. Make sure no yolks get into the whites.
- In a large mixing bowl beat the egg whites on a high speed until soft peaks form.
- Gradually, add the granulated sugar, beating well after each addition. (Basically, you're making a meringue. When stiff peaks form, you've beaten them enough. Remove from mixing bowl and set aside.)
- In a mixing bowl beat the egg yolks on a high speed until they are thick and lemon colored.
- Very carefully, fold the egg yolk mixture into the meringue. I use a spatula.
- Gently fold in the flour, salt and baking powder mixture.
- Gradually fold in the 2 tbl. of melted butter and the two extracts.
- Pour over pineapple, cherries and pecans in skillet.
- Bake for 30-35 minutes until the cake springs back when you press down gently in the center.

When finished, cool for 8 minutes on a cooling rack. Take a knife and run it around the edges to release it. Place a plate on top of the skillet and quickly invert it. It's good warm or cold.

Pralines

This recipe is one of the earliest my grandmother and mother taught me. And, ironically, it's the same one we use at the New Orleans School of Cooking.

Before we begin, I have to give you the advice passed down to me. You will need a pot with a heavy bottom (4 - 4 1/2 qt. size), a wooden spoon with a narrow bowl, parchment paper, wax paper (protect your counter by putting newspaper underneath the wax paper), tin foil, marble or granite slab. Butter the top of all the surfaces (except the parchment and wax papers). A glass measuring cup filled halfway up with cold water. One more thing, a timer and candy thermometer come in handy (read the directions for the proper use of a candy thermometer). I don't trust the thermometer entirely so I always use the soft ball test. Regardless, you must know the syrup is 238 - 240°. The soft ball test assures this. – Harriet

INGREDIENTS

6 tbl. butter (salted or unsalted)

1 tsp. vanilla

½ cup whole milk

1½ cups granulated sugar

¾ cup light brown sugar

1½ cups pecans (whole or pieces)

INSTRUCTIONS

- Place everything in the pot on medium heat. Stir to combine. It is not necessary to stir the entire time, just once in a while.
- When the syrup boils, set the timer for 3 minutes. Put the candy thermometer in the syrup at this time.
- When syrup mixture reaches 238 - 240°(soft ball stage) test a small amount of syrup in cold water. Drop a small amount of the syrup into the cold water and slide it up the side of the cup. If it stays up, it's ready to go to the next step - cooling down.
- Begin beating the mixture. Tilt the pot and stir vigorously. As you stir, the mixture will begin to thicken. You will hear a soft rubbing sound similar to rubbing 2 hands together.
- Now it's time to begin dropping the mixture off the spoon (any size you like) one spoon at a time. A healthy tablespoon of syrup will make about 36 - 48 small pralines. Let the candy cool down. Store in an air tight container. Oh! So good!

Praline Mini Muffins

Pralines are the candy of New Orleans. No other city in the United States can claim the praline. There are praline makers all over the French Quarter making them every which way. The New Orleans School of Cooking makes some of the best pralines in the city from scratch everyday. I have the pleasure of demonstrating their recipe for the visitors often. Delicious!

The Praline Mini Muffin has the same flavor as the praline and they are addictive. It's the flavor of the pecans and the sugar that really gives you the essence of a New Orleans candy. I love this twist on the flavors. And as a mini muffin, you can serve these at brunch or as a quick snack.

I encourage you to use this recipe to get some of your younger family members interested in cooking and baking. It's one of the first recipes my daughters, Suzanne, Katherine, and Victoria learned to make. – Harriet

INGREDIENTS

- 1 cup brown sugar (dark or light), packed
- 1 cup pecans, finely chopped
- ½ cup all purpose flour
- 1½ sticks butter, melted
- 2 eggs, beaten
- ¼ tsp. salt

INSTRUCTIONS

- Preheat oven to 350°.
- Mix all ingredients together and spoon into well greased mini muffin tins. (I use Bakers Joy to spray tins).
- Bake 15-20 min. until golden brown
- When ready to come out of the oven, immediately turn over and remove muffins from tin. Cool on a wire rack and serve.

HINT: I only make this recipe in a mini muffin tin. The cook time above ensures they come out perfect every time. Also, if you wash the tins right before filling, make sure you dry them thoroughly. DO NOT USE MUFFIN PAPER LINERS!

This recipe makes 24.

ingredients

1 cup pecans, chopped
1 box yellow cake mix*
1 (3 oz.) box small vanilla
  instant pudding
4 large eggs
½ cup cold water
½ cup oil
½ cup good rum (dark or
  light) 80 proof

rum sauce:

1 stick butter
¼ cup water
1 cup granulated sugar
½ cup rum

Rum Cake

My mother and I lived with my maternal grandmother in her home on Constance & Octavia streets during WWII. Down the street lived the Cortese family. Mr. Sam Cortesse made and sold Roman Candy from his mule drawn wagon. The taffy candy is flavored with vanilla, strawberry or chocolate. One can still see the mule drawn cart on the streets of New Orleans usually in the picturesque Audubon Park area in Uptown New Orleans.

One time while Anne & I were demonstrating cooking at a home show, we had an opportunity to sample the Cortese family's new product, Roman Candy Rum. And to our delight it tasted exactly like the Roman Candy! Needless to say, we both bought a bottle.

This rum cake is my go to cake for holidays and when I need a dessert to take to a friend's house. Make this in a Bundt pan. You are going to drizzle the hot rum sauce over the cake while it is still in the pan. It's so easy to put in the car and go. When you get where you are going, then you flip it out of the pan! Everyone will be thrilled. – Harriet

INSTRUCTIONS

- Pre-heat oven to 325°.
- Grease and flour a 10 inch Bundt or tube pan.
- Sprinkle chopped nuts over bottom of pan.
- Mix all ingredients together and pour over nuts.
- Bake for 1 hour, check cake with a toothpick after 50-55 min. When finished do not unmold.
- Cool on wire rack and follow directions below for adding sauce while cake is hot from oven.

RUM SAUCE:

- Combine all ingredients in saucepan, bring to boil for 1 minute.
- Be attentive, the sauce will boil over quickly.
- While cake is still hot and still in the pan, puncture all over with a serving fork.
- Pour hot rum sauce over cake, do this slowly and carefully.
- Let cake cool in pan, then invert on a serving plate.

*If you use a cake mix with the pudding already added, omit the pudding in the above recipe. Use 3 eggs, not 4. Reduce oil from ½ cup to ⅓ cup.

INGREDIENTS

1 (12 oz.) can Pet Milk
(evaporated milk)
2 tbl. vanilla
½ cup granulated sugar (or
more to taste)
2 pints fresh strawberries,
chop into small chunks

Strawberry Ice Cream

When strawberry season would come around, Grandma would make this really easy strawberry ice cream. I can still see it in the freezer in a metal meatloaf style pan. I make mine in a Tupperware bread container. With the availability of frozen strawberries, you can make this anytime of the year. Although I've never done it, I bet you could do this with almost any kind of fruit. – Anne

Instructions

- This is going to sound strange but this is what you do. Pour Pet milk into a plastic container and place in the freezer. Set your timer for 45 minutes. Every 45 minutes, stir the Pet milk until you eventually get it to a slushy state. You don't want the milk to freeze solid. You simply need it to be a somewhat frozen consistency.
- Again, another strange process - but do it. Place the slushy milk, vanilla and sugar in a mixing bowl and whip it on high speed until it becomes fluffy. Taste for sweetness. If you need more sugar then add it in the beginning. It will double in size - absolutely amazing!
- Then, gently fold in the strawberries.
- Transfer to container for freezing. Just like when you were freezing the Pet milk, you're going to do the same thing. Every 45 minutes, stir the entire mixture - that way you're making sure the strawberries are staying in suspension.

HINT: This ice cream does tend to melt quickly - so be prepared.

INGREDIENTS

2 baked deep dish pie shells
2 pints fresh strawberries,
  (not frozen) sliced thinly
3 tbl. cornstarch
1 cup granulated sugar
1½ cups water
1 (6 oz) pkg. strawberry
  Jell-O
1 pint heavy cream
  whipped or Cool Whip

Strawberry Pie

When Pontchatoula, Louisiana strawberries come into season, Louisianians scramble to find ways to enjoy them. For those that don't know, Pontchatuoula is one of the premier spots in the United States for strawberries. They have a wonderful festival and have built a whole town's reputation around the beloved strawberry. Pontchatoula is just an hour's drive from downtown New Orleans.

This is such an easy pie to make. We top it with mounds of whipping cream (naturally) but Cool Whip would work as well. - *Anne*

INSTRUCTIONS

- Bake pie shell according to directions. Cool.
- Divide the sliced strawberries evenly between the pie shells.
- In a small saucepan, combine cornstarch, sugar and water. Stir continuously on a medium high heat for about 10 minutes until the mixture begins to thicken.
- Remove from heat and stir in the Jell-O.
- Pour the mixture evenly between the two pie shells. Place in refrigerator uncovered until Jell-O sets, about 4 hours.
- Finish with whipped topping of your choice.

10

a LITTLE SOMETHING EXTRA

Lagniappe

Fish Sauces

ALMONDINE SAUCE:

Like most great French sauces there is a base and then you create from there. Almondine is basically a browned butter sauce with almonds. I love the crunch from the almonds with the crispy fish. - *Anne*

MEUNIÈRE SAUCE (PRONOUNCED MUN-YARE)

As with many of my sauces, I've learned to cook them ahead of time so they're ready to serve when the meat or fish is freshly cooked. Just think ahead a little and plan the flow. You can keep this on the backburner while you fry the fish. - *Anne*

INGREDIENTS

ALMONDINE SAUCE:
1½ stick butter* (plain or unsalted)
¾ cup sliced almonds
1 tbl. Worcestershire sauce
1 tbl. lemon juice**
pinch cayenne (Yes! Use it.)

MEUNIÈRE SAUCE:
1½ stick butter* (plain or unsalted)
1 tbl. Worcestershire sauce (remember to shake the bottle)
1 tbl. lemon juice**
Pinch cayenne
1 tbl. capers drained, optional

INSTRUCTIONS

ALMONDINE SAUCE:
• Melt the butter in a skillet over a medium fire.
• Add the almonds and sauté until medium brown color.
• Add the remaining ingredients and stir.
• Keep warm until ready to pour over fish.

MEUNIÈRE SAUCE:
• In a medium saucepan melt the butter, then add the rest of the ingredients.
• Serve warm.

*The original way was to clarify the butter. I don't do that. It's too much trouble.
**If you prefer either sauce a little more tart, then increase the lemon juice.

All About Shrimp

In New Orleans we love our locally caught shrimp! We eat them boiled, fried, baked, barbequed, in soups, gumbos, in stuffings and in mouth watering entrées. The next few recipes will guide you through boiling, presentations and sauces.

We have many bottled liquids as well as powdered mixes available to us for boiling seafood. They're all good… it is basically what you grew up with. A very popular brand in New Orleans is called Zatarain's (that's what I use).

Basically, follow the directions and you'll be fine. Just remember this - boiling seafood takes a lot of salt. If it seems like too much in the directions, do it anyway. These companies are pros at this.

Another important thing, particularly with shrimp, is that they are easily overcooked, so use a timer. I always mix the shrimp in tons of ice cubes when I take them out of the pot. We boil our shrimp with the heads and shells on, unless we need to make a stock. – Anne

Boiled Shrimp:

INGREDIENTS
1 lb. of shrimp
1½ gal. of water
Seasoning mix.

INSTRUCTIONS
- Bring to a rolling boil and boil for five minutes.
- Add shrimp, stir, and return to the boil.
- Boil shrimp 1-2 minutes (yes!), turn off fire; soak 2-5 minutes, depending on the size of the shrimp.
- Drain and plunge into ice to cool down.
- Nothing to it!

Classic Boiled Shrimp Presentation

INGREDIENTS
36 shrimp, 16-20 size boiled with heads removed, peeled and chilled (tails intact is optional)
½ head lettuce of your choice, shredded
1 lemon, sliced in 6 wedges

INSTRUCTIONS
- In a non-reactive bowl, combine sauce (recipe follows) and peeled shrimp. Gently mix to coat shrimp thoroughly. Cover and chill for 3 to 4 hours in the refrigerator
- Place 6 serving plates in refrigerator to chill.
- Divide the lettuce among the six serving dishes.
- Arrange 6 shrimp on each plate and top with a generous dollop of sauce.
- Garnish with a lemon wedge and serve chilled.
- Serves 6

All About Shrimp

Cocktail Sauce

When we were growing up, practically every restaurant served shrimp cocktail. The sauce is basically the same thing we use for raw oysters. The dish consists of boiled, peeled shrimp in a smooth red sauce served over finely shredded lettuce. More of a tomato base sauce, it was our alternative to Remoulade. Not as heavy but rich and delicious. It definitely has a kick to it.

INGREDIENTS

- 1 cup ketchup
- 1 tbl. horseradish
- 1 tbl. lemon juice, freshly squeezed
- ⅛ tsp. Kosher salt
- dash Worcestershire sauce
- dash hot sauce
- ¼ tsp. crushed red pepper
- 1½ lbs. shrimp, boiled and peeled (tails intact is optional)
- ½ head lettuce of your choice, shredded

INSTRUCTIONS

- Combine all ingredients except lettuce in a non-reactive bowl.
- Chill sauce and follow instructions for classic shrimp presentation.

White Remoulade Sauce

Creole cuisine borrows heavily from classic French cooking traditions. Remoulade is one of the sauces that was part of the repertoire brought over by the French chefs who arrived in New Orleans after the French Revolution. Over the years, New Orleanians have perfected the many recipes that have become hallmarks of our New Orleans dishes. One of the standout sauces we New Orleanians eat on a regular basis is remoulade sauce. There are two kinds of remoulades, red and white. – *Anne*

White Remoulade

My father-in-law made this incredible white remoulade, a more French rendition. His recipe has the classic flavor profile, and is my favorite version. I think of remoulade as the soulmate to our wonderful fried and boiled seafood and in particular the popular New Orleans own Shrimp Remoulade.

Ingredients

- 1 cup mayonnaise
- ⅓ cup Creole mustard (similar to Dijon coarse mustard)
- 1½ tsp. lemon juice, freshly squeezed
- ¼ cup green onions, finely chopped
- dash Worcestershire sauce
- ½ tsp. hot sauce
- Dash cayenne
- 1-2 tbl. horseradish sauce
- 1½ lbs. shrimp, boiled and peeled (tails intact is optional)
- ½ head lettuce of your choice, shredded

Instructions

- Combine all ingredients except lettuce in a non-reactive bowl.
- Chill sauce and follow instructions for classic shrimp presentation.

All the ingredients can be adjusted to your taste. Perfect example is the horseradish. Start with one tablespoon and adjust up if needed.

Red Remoulade Sauce

Red Remoulade

I'm a graduate of an all-girls Catholic school here in New Orleans run by the Ursuline nuns. Let me tell you-strict. You bet! So when I took a position at a public school in the 1970's let's just say eye opening doesn't even begin to explain that year. I sought sanctuary and sanity by taking up pottery and actually became quite a successful production potter. I sold my wares at fairs and to the Blue Roof Pottery Shop in New Orleans run by a charming lady named Bernice. Bernice was a fabulous cook and the source of this recipe. As a matter of fact, when Bernice died, her obituary in the newspaper even mentioned that she was known for her Remoulade sauce. That's New Orleans for you! This classic red version, which is more of the New Orleans style remoulade, is my husband Alan's favorite. *- Anne*

INGREDIENTS

- 1 bunch green onions, finely chopped
- ½ tsp. black pepper
- 1 stalk celery, finely chopped
- 3 tbl. parsley, finely chopped
- ⅓ cup white vinegar
- ¼ cup paprika
- ⅔ cup olive oil
- 4 tbl. Creole mustard (similar to Dijon Mustard coarse ground)
- 2 tbl. horseradish sauce
- 1 tsp. lemon juice, freshly squeezed
- 1½ lbs. shrimp, boiled and peeled (tails intact is optional)
- ½ head lettuce of your choice, shredded

INSTRUCTIONS

- Combine all ingredients except lettuce in a non-reactive bowl.
- Chill sauce and follow instructions for classic shrimp presentation.

Puppy Chow

My granddaughter, Barrett (Tommy's child), went away to camp a few summers ago. She came back with this snack that she learned to make in Mentone, Alabama. It's fun to make and good to nibble on. – Anne

INGREDIENTS

1 (8 oz.) bag chocolate chips (milk or semi-sweet)
½ cup peanut butter
1 (8 oz.) bag Chex mix
1 cup confectioners sugar

INSTRUCTIONS

• Melt chocolate in a double boiler.
• Remove from fire.
• Mix the peanut butter into the chocolate.
• Pour over the Chex mix, stirring the entire time.
• Sprinkle with confectioners sugar, a little at a time until it looks polka dotted.
• Cool down.

HINT: If it is hot outside, put in refrigerator until it is no longer sticky. I can't tell you how long it will keep because we always "kill it" in one evening!

Tiger Sauce

My daughter Beth is a very talented cook. She can taste something once and can pretty much copy it. This is one such recipe. It is wonderful over crab cakes, fried eggplant rounds, boiled shrimp, crabmeat and pretty much anything you can think of. It has a very definite kick because of the horseradish. – *Anne*

INGREDIENTS

- ¼ tsp. cayenne pepper to taste
- ¼ cup granulated sugar
- 3-5 tbl. horseradish in a jar (depends on how much "kick" you want)
- 3 tbl. white vinegar
- 2 cups mayonnaise
- ¼ cup Karo syrup
- ½ lemon, squeezed

INSTRUCTIONS

- Mix together and refrigerate.

Beef and Italian Sausage Dressing

This recipe gives you four pounds of meaty goodness. And, for goodness sakes, I think it's been around longer than my children. That's the truth. I can't remember where this recipe came from, I only know that you can use it every which way from Lasagna, stuffed vegetables, stuffed pasta shells and meat sauce for spaghetti. It has made my life very easy in the kitchen. The flavors can be easily enhanced with Creole flavors or Italian flavors by just adjusting the seasoning. The versatility of this recipe serves as a reminder that you can easily guide one recipe into many uses. *- Harriet*

INGREDIENTS

- 2 tbl. olive oil
- 2 cups onions, finely chopped
- 1 cup celery, finely chopped
- ½ cup green bell pepper, finely chopped
- ½ cup parsley, finely chopped
- ½ cup green onions, finely chopped
- 3 toes (cloves) garlic, finely chopped
- 3 lb. ground chuck (80/20 blend)
- 1½ lb. good tasting Italian sausage, remove from casing
- 2 cups croutons, Italian or Caesar style soaked in warm water to soften.
- 2 tsp. each of dried rosemary (crushed), basil, oregano, fennel seeds or more to your taste
- 2 tsp. Joe's Stuff seasoning

INSTRUCTIONS

- Preheat the pot over a medium fire. Add olive oil to hot pot. When oil is shimmering, add the Trinity (onion, celery, bell pepper).
- Sauté for 5 minutes.
- Add parsley, green onion and garlic.
- Add the meat and sauté until the meat is cooked through and crumbled about 6 minutes.
- As the meat is browning, add the croutons (squeeze out the water first).
- Add the dried herbs and Joe's Stuff seasoning. Stir to blend well.
- Continue to cook until meat is no longer pink.
- Taste and adjust seasoning.

Bordelaise Sauce

Bordelaise sauce is great over steaks. Here's how it is done in New Orleans. A totally different approach from other cities. – *Anne*

Rough chop garlic. The amount depends on how potent you want it. For Alan and me, I'll usually use about 8 big toes (cloves). Melt the butter (about ½ a stick) in a saucepan. Add the rough chopped garlic and cook on a low fire for a few minutes until the garlic softens. You don't want to brown the garlic or the butter.

When serving, simply sprinkle a little finely chopped parsley over the top of the steak and drizzle the sauce over that. I can't guarantee you won't reek of garlic, but that will help keep the vampires away!

VARIATION:

My sisters prefer to do it the way my mother did. They allow the butter to sit out on the counter and soften. They then add finely chopped garlic and finely chopped parsley to the butter and mix together. They can easily adjust the garlic potency that way. It definitely has a more intense garlic flavor because you're using raw garlic. Spread as much or as little as you want on your steak.

ingredients

1 (12 oz.) bag fresh
   cranberries
1 (15 oz.) box raisins,
   (Muscat if possible)*
1 medium thin skin orange,
   remove seeds, grind skins
   and all
1½ tsp. ginger
1½ tsp. cloves
1½ tsp. cinnamon
 ½ cup cider vinegar
3½ cups granulated sugar

Cranberry Relish

I still have the scrap of paper with the original recipe that was given to me at a Christmas party. I cooked many pots of this relish over the years. It's one of my favorite recipes. – *Harriet*

INSTRUCTIONS

- Put all ingredients in a Dutch oven.
- Bring to a boil. Reduce to a simmer.
- Simmer until berries break up, about 30 min.

DO NOT OVER COOK.

Ladle into sterilized jars and cap, or put into container to be used immediately for lunch or dinner.

*The recipe calls for Muscat raisins with seeds. Lately, I cannot find Muscat raisins. Today I use regular raisins dark or golden without seeds. When you are selecting the orange, pick one with a thin skin. Have fun and enjoy.

Gravies New Orleans Style

I love gravy! My children and grandchildren are gravy lovers also. We all grew up eating gravy on rice, potatoes and meat. In fact, in our family we thought of gravy as a beverage.

Funny story about gravy and one of my grandsons, Jack (Timothy's son). Jack must have been about 6 or 7. He is a teaser just like his father. He'll get this devilish glint in his eye a lot of times so you know he's up to something. It was Christmas Day. We've got a beautiful dinner laid out, etc. In our home everyone serves themselves from a long kitchen counter - left to right (kindergarten training). Even for our everyday meals we serve like this. Jack had just finished loading up his plate. As he walked into the dining room I saw "the look" in his eyes. I glanced down at his plate - NO GRAVY! I said, "Jack, you forgot the gravy." He said, "No, I didn't. I don't like gravy anymore." I replied, "Every Leonhard loves gravy. I took his plate, cut in line, and added gravy to the rice and turkey. He gobbled it up. – *Anne*

TWO KINDS OF GRAVY

In New Orleans there are basically two kinds of gravy - red and brown - and that's it. The red is obvious - meatballs, lasagna, daube and the list goes on. Brown gravies accompany our rice, potatoes, roasts, turkey, steaks, etc.

ROUX BASED GRAVY

First of all, you'll need a good skillet. Personally, I love cast iron – it's indestructible. Aluminum and stainless are fine also. Just avoid skillets that have rivets on the inside of the bowl. Before making the roux everything has to be ready to go. First, sauté the trinity, then set aside. Make sure the liquid is warm otherwise when you add it to the roux it may lump up.

Heat the oil on a medium heat until it begins to simmer. Carefully add the flour quickly and begin whisking the entire time. Gradually, the color of the roux will go through color changes – blonde, beige, light brown sugar and finally peanut butter color. It's going to smell like it's burning towards the end, but it's not unless you see black flecks. If that happens it's ruined – throw it out, clean the skillet, and start again. When the roux is the color you need, immediately pour it over the sautéed vegetables. Then add the warmed stock.

One more thing – NO DISTRACTIONS! No children, no cell phones, no texting, etc.! I know I sound old fashioned – but you've got to give your full attention to the procedure. After you feel comfortable doing this – then it's up to you. But in the beginning – NO!

RED GRAVY

This recipe makes a lot. The beauty of it is that it can be frozen in portions so you always have it on hand. Also, it's rather thick so if you need it for a dish with thinner gravy, you just add water. One other thing—you have to devote half a day to this because it entails a lot of cooking down. *- Anne*

INGREDIENTS

Olive oil for browning meats and onions
2 pieces pork (I use country style ribs)
1 small chuck roast
Joe's Stuff seasoning to taste
4 medium onions, finely chopped
1 entire head garlic, finely chopped
1 (28 oz.) can whole or diced tomatoes
8 (6 oz.) cans tomato paste
10 cups water
3 bay leaves
2 tbl. Italian seasonings
⅛-¼ cup sugar (or more), not to be added until close to the end (optional)

INSTRUCTIONS

- In a large stockpot put enough oil to coat the bottom.
- Season meat with Joe's Stuff seasoning.
- On high heat, brown the meats and set aside. If you need more oil for the onions, add some.
- On a high heat sauté the onions until lightly browned. Then add the garlic and cook a few minutes more.
- Drain the tomatoes and set aside. Place the juice in the pot and reduce until the liquid evaporates. It will stick to the pan a little.
- Add the tomatoes and cook awhile until they begin to break up.
- Lower the fire and add the tomato paste and begin to cook A LONG WHILE. Eventually the paste will darken. Be careful, it will begin to stick to the bottom of the pot. I've found the best tool to work with is a wooden spatula. You really need to keep an eye on the pot!
- Then, add water, blend. Add the remaining ingredients.
- Bring to a boil, reduce heat as low as possible and cook for at least 3- 4 hours.
- You will need to stir often--- this is not a dish that can cook by itself. It is thick so it has a tendency to stick.
- Adjust seasonings toward the end. Sometimes you'll need to add sugar to cut the sharpness of the tomatoes.
- When the gravy is finished remove the roast and ribs. I use that meat for Sloppy Joes and po-boy sandwiches.
- Freeze in portions.

ingredients

OLIVE SALAD:*
Add these ingredients to the Itailian Olive Salad recipe on pg. 48

- ½ cup chopped carrots
- ½ cup cauliflower florets
- ½ cup red bell pepper, finely chopped
- ½ (3.5 oz) jar drained capers
- 1 tsp. dried oregano
- ½ tsp. dried basil
  pinch red pepper flakes
- 1 toe (clove) garlic, finely chopped
- ⅓ cup additional olive oil
- 2 tbl. roasted sesame seeds

SANDWICH:
- 10" round loaf of course textured bread with sesame seeds on top
- ¼ lb. Genoa salami, thinly sliced (divided in half)
- ¼ lb. mortadella (a large Italian pork sausage, thinly sliced)
- ⅛ lb. mozzarella, thinly sliced
- ¼ lb. hot capicola ham, thinly sliced
- ⅛ lb. provolone, thinly sliced

Muffuletta Sandwich

Of all the little Sicilian grocery stores that dotted the quarter through the 40's – only one remains – Central Grocery. It is a New Orleans icon. They lay claim to inventing the muffuletta, an Italian equivalent to the po-boy sandwich. The recipe takes the olive salad recipe and adds a lot more goodies. It is served on a huge round bun with sesame seeds on top. You slice it into 4 pieces and imagine you're in Sicily. – *Anne*

INSTRUCTIONS

OLIVE SALAD:*
- Mix all ingredients and marinate for several days in the refrigerator.
- To roast the sesame seeds simply put the seeds in a skillet and heat on low fire, shaking occasionally until lightly brown, about 4 - 5 minutes.

SANDWICH:
- Cut the bread in half lengthwise.
- Brush the inside of both halves of the bread with extra virgin olive oil from the marinated salad.

Begin assembling in this order:
1/2 of the salami
mortadella
sliced mozzarella
sliced capicola
sliced provolone
remainder of salami
top generously with olive salad

Robin Family Pepper Jelly

My aunt Eleanor gave us her pepper jelly recipe in the early 1960's. Daddy and Momma fell in love with it and it's been a family tradition since. Momma served it with sweet pickled meat and red beans and rice. Daddy was a hunter and during duck season Momma would serve it with wild roasted duck. That's how pepper jelly got its start in my family.

The Robin Family Pepper Jelly, along with my Cranberry Relish, really became legendary in the 1970's when a few of the St. Catherine of Siena School mothers got together and created Holiday Hobbies! We created our own holiday boutique to raise money by selling our handiwork which funded our gift giving. It was a huge hit. For many of us, we were busy raising kids so it was a resourceful way for us to earn money. Well, I'm not crafty but it dawned on me that I could make the jelly and the relish! I made 100 jars of each of the jelly and relish and sold out every year. These recipes are that good. – Harriet

INGREDIENTS

1½ cups ground red green bell pepper and juice*

½ cups ground jalapeño pepper and juices*

13 cups granulated sugar

3 cups apple cider vinegar

2 tsp. salt

2 pouches Certo (1 whole box)

12 half pint sterilized jars (the dishwasher will do this for you)

INSTRUCTIONS

• Clean peppers, remove seeds and ribs. Wear gloves when cleaning the hot peppers.
• Wash hands very well after this prep work.
• Mix first 5 ingredients including the pepper juice in a heavy bottom Dutch oven.
• Bring to a hard boil and boil 5 minutes.
• Cool for 10 minutes.
• Add the Certo, mix well, pour into sterilized jars and loosely cover.
• Stir when partially cool to keep pepper particles from sinking to the bottom of the jar.

Back in the 1960's I used a hand grinder, today the peppers are put into my food processor.

*Remove seeds and ribs

Spiced Christmas Pecans

I lived in the French Quarter for ten years with the greatest neighbors you could ever wish for. We had so much fun. And, we took every opportunity to have stoop parties that included cocktails and people watching. My neighbor, David, would make these and pass them out for Christmas gifts for everyone. The rest of the year we made sure to have them on hand because they are that good. A famous stoop recipe for sure. And, oh, how good! - *Harriet*

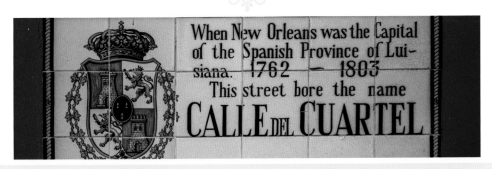

When New Orleans was the Capital of the Spanish Province of Luisiana. 1762 - 1803 This street bore the name CALLE DEL CUARTEL

Ingredients

- 3 qt. boiling water
- 1 lb. large pecan halves
- 1 cup confectioners sugar
- Cooking oil for frying
- 2 tbl. Joe's Stuff seasoning

Instructions

- In a medium size Dutch oven heat oil to 350°.
- Blanch the pecans in boiling water for 2 - 3 minutes.
- Drain pecans well and toss pecans in sugar to coat.
- When the oil is ready, add the pecans to oil in small batches, careful not to overcrowd the pan.
- Cook for 1 - 2 minutes.
- Remove pecans with slotted spoon to cookie sheet lined with paper towel to drain.
- Season with Joe's Stuff seasoning while warm.
- Once cool, break apart and store in airtight jars.
- Delicious in salad or just enjoy as a snack.

Sweet Hot Pickles

There are pickles and then there are these pickles. The best you ever made. These pickles are soooo good, but give me a break. I have to wait 30 days!
- *Harriet*

INGREDIENTS

1 gal. jar whole dill pickles

10 toes (cloves) garlic, at least a whole head smacked with knife to break open.

1 lb. carrots, peeled and cut into 3" long sticks

10 lb. granulated sugar

1 (6 oz.) bottle Crystal hot sauce

INSTRUCTIONS

- Discard pickle juice. Keep jar. Slice or cube pickles.
- Pack jar with pickles, garlic toes, and carrot sticks.
- Pour sugar over pickles. Add hot sauce.
- Seal with original lid and make sure lid is tightly secured.

Store pickle jar upside down on a pie plate or pan with at least a 1" lip in a cool, dark place. Turn once a day for 30 days. Your pantry will be just fine

Enjoy!

Nectar Syrup

Have you ever wondered how Nectar syrup is made? You'll be surprised how easy it is to make. We use it in ice cream, sodas, on snowballs and so on. - *Anne*

INGREDIENTS

4 cups granulated sugar
3 cups water
1 cup Pet milk
(evaporated milk)
3 tsp. pure almond
extract
3 tsp. pure vanilla
extract
½-1 tsp. red food coloring
for a pretty shade of
pink

INSTRUCTIONS

- Put the sugar and water in a saucepan and simmer over medium heat until the sugar dissolves, about 5 minutes.
- Remove from fire, stir in the remaining ingredients.
- Cool and refrigerate.

Index

Index

Anne Leonhard

Anne Leonhard is a fourth generation New Orleanian. Her mother, Irene, was 50% French and 50% German. Her father, Sheldon, was 50% Irish and 50% Cajun French (both heritages which he was extremely proud of). So Anne (like most native New Orleanians) is a cultural "gumbo".

In 1964 she married Alan (also a fourth generation and a cultural gumbo) and moved to Springfield, Missouri where he was a professor. While there, she received her degree from Southwest Missouri State College in elementary education. They returned to New Orleans in 1966 and have remained ever since. Together they have three children and five grandchildren.

Anne taught kindergarten for most of her professional career. Upon retiring in 1993, she became a licensed tour guide giving walking tours of the French Quarter and Garden District, as well as bus tours of the entire city. She delved into the history and architecture and hasn't stopped sharing it since. She remains an active guide to this day. As a result of her endeavors for The Friends of the Cabildo in 1997, she was awarded "The Golden Shoe" award.

Terry Thibeau

In 1999, Anne was invited to become a lecturer for an education travel program, Road Scholars (formerly called Elderhotel). She continues to work with this organization today.

Then, in 2002 a new career began, still in the teaching field - but this time teaching guests from all over the U.S. and the world, how to cook New Orleans foods! In 2015 Anne won a national cooking contest on the Food Network – entitled "Clash of the Grandmas."

Together with her cooking partner and good friend, Harriet Robin, she has appeared on numerous local television programs and the nationally syndicated Steve Harvey Show. Steve Harvey coined the phrase "The New Orleans Grannies" and that titled remains with them today.

Harriet Robin

Harriet Robin is fourth generation New Orleanian. Her father was 100% Cajun; her mother was 100% Irish. That ancestry has helped her be the cook she is today. Harriet's Cajun "Maw-Maw" encouraged her to make a dark, dark roux. Her Irish grandmother would say, "put a color on it (meaning Kitchen Bouquet) and let's go". She can still hear both grandmothers in her head, but she wound up doing it her way. "Miss Harriet", Harriet's mother, was an excellent cook but she had a career. So basically Harriet learned to cook over the telephone - "What does it look like?....keep going."

Harriet graduated from St. Mary's Dominican College with a degree in Food and Nutrition. After college she left New Orleans to do a one-year internship in the great Northern city of Cincinnati, Ohio. On the day she arrived, the Ohio River was frozen over! Being from the south, she cried out "What have I done to myself!"

Harriet returned home, married and promptly had a family (five children in five years!). When all the children were in school she took up her career as Production and Purchasing Dietician at a local hospital for 30+ years.

She worked with a team of talented men and women who cooked phenomenal meals for patients and staff from scratch every day.

After retiring, Harriet moved to the French Quarter and began a whole new life. She became a tour guide which she continues to this day. Several years after that she found her way to The New Orleans School of Cooking where everything fell into place. That association has allowed her to demonstrate cooking on local television, countless festivals and the Steve Harvey Show on National television seven times.

Together with her cooking partner and friend from childhood, Anne Leonhard, they are known as "The New Orleans Grannies".

Terry Thibeau